MW00398740

dlife
JOURNAL
OLD TESTAMENT 1

Property of:

_____

Published by Life Bible Study

Life Bible Study LLC is a Christian publisher serving churches and Christian communities in order to advance the Gospel of Jesus Christ, making disciples as we go.

© 2018 Life Bible Study
D-Life Journal: Old Testament 1 by Dr. Bill Wilks
Publisher Dr. John Herring

All rights reserved. No part of this publication may be reproduced, stored in a retrieval system, or transmitted in any form or by any means, electronic, mechanical, photocopying, recording, or otherwise, without the prior permission of Life Bible Study. Address all correspondence to Life Bible Study LLC, 5184 Caldwell Mill Road, Suite 204-221, Hoover, AL 35244.

ISBN-13: 978-1-63204-079-4
ISBN-10: 1-63204-079-4
LifeBibleStudy.com

Unless otherwise noted, all Scripture taken from the Holy Bible, NEW INTERNATIONAL VERSION®, NIV® Copyright © 1973, 1978, 1984, 2011 by Biblica, Inc.® Used by permission. All rights reserved worldwide.

Printed in the United States of America
1 2 3 4 5 6 / 24 23 22 21 20 19

TABLE OF CONTENTS

INTRODUCTION

Jesus charged His disciples with making disciples (Matthew 28:19), baptizing in His name and teaching them His commandments. That charge is just as relevant today as it was to the first-century church. Becoming a disciple is more than being saved and baptized. Becoming a disciple involves learning to follow God by carefully and diligently studying God's Word and then by intentionally living God's Word for others to see.

Discipleship is a journey and life-long process. It involves daily seeking to know God's heart, studying God's Word, and then living out God's expectations. It is not an easy journey, but it is more rewarding than any other endeavor in this life.

D-Life Journal is a discipleship tool that can be used as a guide for personal spiritual growth or in a discipleship group. Groups can begin with as few as three to five members. New groups should be started when a group enrollment reaches eight. To begin a discipleship group, consider creating diversity within the group, such as:

- New believers, who can benefit by connecting in discipleship to other believers.

- Unbelievers and the unchurched who are open to hearing about Jesus.

- Multi-generational believers, who bring different life stages and different spiritual journeys into the group.

- Believers struggling in life with issues such as drug abuse, depression, and gender identification, who will benefit from having the support and accountability of other believers.

HOW TO LEAD A D-LIFE GROUP:

- **Fellowship Time** – Create fellowship within the group wherever it meets—a coffee shop, café, home, park, school, or church. Share coffee, a snack, or a meal.

- **Accountability Time** – Create accountability each week by asking if group members read their Bibles daily. Lead them to share some application points written in their notes.

- **Prayer Time**– Develop an on-going emphasis on prayer, with members taking responsibility for leading the group in prayer, praying for specific prayer requests, and praying for revival in our land.

- **Tell the Story** – Assign a member in the group each week to tell the biblical story or paraphrase the passage to be studied in his or her own words.

- **Read the Story** – Assign another member in the group to read the passage to be studied from the Bible. See if anything was left out of the storytelling.

- **Facilitate Bible Study** – Assign another member in your group to facilitate the Bible study using the questions provided in the weekly study guide.

  When facilitating, use the study guide questions with intention. When time is an issue, use only 3 to 5 questions and work to intentionally involve all group members in discussion. Keep the discussion on point. Be truthful, positive, and transparent. Clearly address theological issues when necessary. Be sensitive to the Holy Spirit.

- **Ministry Planning Time** – Spend a few minutes planning for your next ministry project. You will do one ministry and evangelism project every two months.

- **Weekly Assignments** –Assign tasks for the next week to different members of the group: lead in prayer, tell the story, read the story, and facilitate the Bible study.

S-P-A-C-E BIBLE STUDY METHOD

A major goal of D-Life is to lead people to develop a life long habit of daily Bible reading. This alone is life changing. Each day we want to make SPACE in our hearts for God's Word by writing down one personal application point from our daily Bible reading assignments. We make **S-P-A-C-E** by asking five simple questions as we read each chapter. Ask, is there a:

- **S**in to confess?
- **P**romise to claim?
- **A**ttitude to change?
- **C**ommand to obey?
- **E**xample to follow?

In each chapter you will find an answer to at least one of these question. Ask God to give you a personal word as you read. Let the Holy Spirit speak to your heart. As you ask these questions, let God show you a personal point of application. Psalm 119:18 is a great prayer to pray, "Open my eyes, that I may behold wondrous things out of your law."

When God speaks to your heart, you want to write it down. In your journal, circle the appropriate letter in the acrostic **S-P-A-C-E** that relates to your application point and write a brief note reflecting your thoughts. For example, in John 3:16, you may see a "Promise to claim." Circle the letter "P" and then you may write something like: "What a great promise to claim! God loves me and has given me eternal life through faith in His Son. Thank you God for your incredible gift to me."

It's helpful to have a certain time and place where you meet alone with God each day for prayer and Bible reading. Make your daily time alone with God a major priority in your life.

Taken from Rick Warren's Bible Study Methods: Twelve Ways You Can Unlock God's Word by Rick Warren Copyright © 2006 by Rick Warren. Use by permission of Zondervan.

THE MINISTRY OF D-LIFE

To make disciples like Jesus, we must personally train our disciples to do the work of ministry and evangelism "outside the walls" of the church. This is an important part of living the D-Life.

Therefore, every D-Group must be committed to do the work of ministry and evangelism. We cannot disciple others through fellowship and Bible study alone. We MUST be willing to go outside the walls of the church and share in the work of ministry and evangelism together.

THE MINIMUM GOAL OF EVERY D-GROUP is to work together on **one** community ministry and evangelism project every **two** months. This means that every D-Group will participate in a minimum of **six** ministry projects each year. This is a reasonable expectation and an absolute essential for making genuine disciples.

Planning for ministry projects should be a regular part of weekly D-Group meetings. We should keep notes about ministry ideas and upcoming projects. Ministry Projects may include things such as feeding the homeless, crashing someone's yard for lawn care, doing a work project at a local school, building a wheelchair ramp, adopting a family for Christmas, prayer walk evangelism, or other creative ideas. The opportunities are endless. D-Groups can even make plans to go on a mission trip together.

The purpose for all D-Group ministry projects is servant evangelism. We want to advance God's Kingdom on earth.

Kyle Martin, with *TIME TO REVIVE* (www.timetorevive.com), teaches a simple and effective approach to servant evangelism involving the following four steps...

- **Love** – Approach an individual and engage in friendly conversation. Our main concern is to show them love. Then ask, *"Is there anything we can pray for you about?"*
- **Listen** – Listen carefully to him or her and show genuine concern.
- **Discern** – Spiritually discern how you should respond to each individual.
- **Respond** – When appropriate, pray with the individual and share the Gospel.

The *TIME TO REVIVE BIBLE* published by LIFE BIBLE STUDY (www.lifebiblestudy.com) is an excellent tool to use for sharing the Gospel. You can also use THE GOSPEL presentation on your D-Life Web App. Simply turn your mobile phone landscape and flip through the Bible verses as you present the Gospel.

USE THE SPACE BELOW TO PLAN AND KEEP A JOURNAL OF YOUR PROJECTS:

D-GROUP MINISTRY PROJECT #1
Date of Project: _____
Journal Notes on Project: _____
_____
_____
_____

D-GROUP MINISTRY PROJECT #2
Date of Project: _____
Journal Notes on Project: _____
_____
_____
_____

D-GROUP MINISTRY PROJECT #3

Date of Project: _____

Journal Notes on Project: _____

_____

_____

_____

D-GROUP MINISTRY PROJECT #4

Date of Project: _____

Journal Notes on Project: _____

_____

_____

_____

D-GROUP MINISTRY PROJECT #5

Date of Project: _____

Journal Notes on Project: _____

_____

_____

_____

D-GROUP MINISTRY PROJECT #6

Date of Project: _____

Journal Notes on Project: _____

_____

_____

_____

WEEK

Weekly Bible Reading: .... Stories from Genesis
Weekly Bible Study: .... Genesis 3:1-13

GENESIS 1:1-31   [CIRCLE ONE: S P A C E]
Personal Study Notes: _____
_____
_____
_____

GENESIS 2:1-24   [CIRCLE ONE: S P A C E]
Personal Study Notes: _____
_____
_____
_____

GENESIS 3:1-24   [CIRCLE ONE: S P A C E]
Personal Study Notes: _____
_____
_____
_____

GENESIS 4:1-16   [CIRCLE ONE: S P A C E]
Personal Study Notes: _____
_____
_____
_____

GENESIS 6:1-22   [CIRCLE ONE: S P A C E]
Personal Study Notes: _____
_____
_____
_____

Read carefully one chapter of the Bible five days a week. In each chapter look for a . . .
Sin to Confess / **P**romise to Claim / **A**ttitude to Change / **C**ommand to Obey / **E**xample to Follow.

THE FALL OF MAN
(GENESIS 3:1-13)

WEEKLY ASSIGNMENTS:

Lead Prayer Time: _____

Tell the Story (Paraphrase): _____

Read the Text: _____

Facilitate Bible Study: _____

DISCUSSION QUESTIONS:

- How do you feel about snakes? What is the closest encounter you have ever had with a snake? Have you ever been bitten by a snake?

- In our story, Eve had a life-changing encounter with a snake in the Garden of Eden. Who was the serpent in Eden's garden (v. 1a)? How was this serpent different than any other beast of the field?

- Do you think Eve thought it was strange that the serpent spoke with her (v. 1b)? Why or why not? What was the first question the serpent raised with Eve? Why is this a "crafty" question?

- Compare Eve's answer to what God actually said in Genesis 2:15-17. How is Eve's answer different from what God actually said (v. 2-3)? Why do you think Eve's answer is different?

- What was the serpent's great lie to Eve (v. 4-5)? Was there any truth to what the serpent said? How should Eve have responded to the serpent?

- With Satan's lies on her mind, what did Eve see when she looked at the forbidden tree (v. 6a)? What did she not see? Read James 1:13-15. How is Eve's experience with the serpent similar to how people are tempted today?

- Why do you think Adam was so easily led by Eve to eat of the fruit (v. 6b)? Why was this a great mistake? How should Adam have responded to Eve? What happened right after Adam and Eve ate of the fruit (v. 7-8)? Why do you think they tried to hide from God? Why can we not hide from God?

- Since God knows everything, why did He ask, "Where are you" (v. 9)? What excuses did Adam and Eve give for eating the fruit (v. 10-12)? In what way is this an *attitude to change*?

- "Where are you" today in your relationship with God? In what ways would you like to grow closer to God? How should we respond to temptation?

PRAYER:

Let's pray for one another today that we will never listen to Satan's lies.

PRAYER REQUESTS:

BI-MONTHLY MISSION PROJECT NOTES:

WEEK  2

Weekly Bible Reading: .... Stories from Genesis
Weekly Bible Study: .... Genesis 12:1-10

GENESIS 7:1-24   [CIRCLE ONE: S P A C E]

Personal Study Notes: _____

_____

_____

_____

GENESIS 8:1-22   [CIRCLE ONE: S P A C E]

Personal Study Notes: _____

_____

_____

_____

GENESIS 9:1-28   [CIRCLE ONE: S P A C E]

Personal Study Notes: _____

_____

_____

_____

GENESIS 11:1-9   [CIRCLE ONE: S P A C E]

Personal Study Notes: _____

_____

_____

_____

GENESIS 12:1-20   [CIRCLE ONE: S P A C E]

Personal Study Notes: _____

_____

_____

_____

Read carefully one chapter of the Bible five days a week. In each chapter look for a . . .
Sin to Confess / **P**romise to Claim / **A**ttitude to Change / **C**ommand to Obey / **E**xample to Follow.

THE CALL OF ABRAHAM
(GENESIS 12:1-10)

WEEKLY ASSIGNMENTS:

Lead Prayer Time: _____

Tell the Story (Paraphrase): _____

Read the Text: _____

Facilitate Bible Study: _____

DISCUSSION QUESTIONS:

- If someone offered you an exotic vacation to a surprise destination, would you go? Why or why not? What might help you want to go?

- In our story, God had special plans for Abram and called him to go out from his country. What specifically did God call Abram to do and what great promises did He give him (v. 1-2)? Why do you think God had special plans for Abram? Why do you think He did not tell Abram where he was going?

- God said to Abram, "In you all the families of the earth shall be blessed" (v. 3). What do you think God meant by this? Read Gal. 3:13-14. In what way is Jesus Christ the Messiah related to this promise?

- How did Abram respond to God's call? Read Heb. 11:8. What does Abram's obedience teach us about his faith? How would you have responded? Who was Lot and why do you think Abram took Lot with him (v. 4-5a)? Was this a breach of God's call? What does this reveal about Abram?

- How old was Abram when he answered God's call (v. 5b)? Why do you think God called him when he was this old? What can we learn from this? How do you think Sarai, Abram's wife, felt about all of this? In what ways might a transition like this put stress on a marriage and a family?

- Where did Abram go and what did he do when he arrived there (v. 5c-6)? What promise did God give Abram when He appeared to him a second time (v. 7a)? At their age and with no offspring, what do you think Abram and Sarai thought about God's promise? What would you think about God's promise?

- After receiving God's promise, why do you think Abram built an altar to the Lord (v. 7b)? How is this an example for us to follow? Why do you think God allowed "a famine" in the land? What things can we learn about Abram's example of following God's will for our lives?

PRAYER:

Let's pray for one another to follow God's will even when it is difficult.

PRAYER REQUESTS:

BI-MONTHLY MISSION PROJECT NOTES:

WEEK

Weekly Bible Reading: .... Stories from Genesis
Weekly Bible Study: .... Genesis 17:1-21

GENESIS 13:1-18   [CIRCLE ONE: S P A C E]
Personal Study Notes: _____

_____

_____

_____

GENESIS 14:1-24   [CIRCLE ONE: S P A C E]
Personal Study Notes: _____

_____

_____

_____

GENESIS 15:1-21   [CIRCLE ONE: S P A C E]
Personal Study Notes: _____

_____

_____

_____

GENESIS 16:1-16   [CIRCLE ONE: S P A C E]
Personal Study Notes: _____

_____

_____

_____

GENESIS 17:1-27   [CIRCLE ONE: S P A C E]
Personal Study Notes: _____

_____

_____

_____

Read carefully one chapter of the Bible five days a week. In each chapter look for a . . .
Sin to Confess / **P**romise to Claim / **A**ttitude to Change / **C**ommand to Obey / **E**xample to Follow.

GOD'S COVENANT REAFFIRMED
(GENESIS 17:1-21)

WEEKLY ASSIGNMENTS:

Lead Prayer Time: _____

Tell the Story (Paraphrase): _____

Read the Text: _____

Facilitate Bible Study: _____

DISCUSSION QUESTIONS:

- Is your name a family name or does it have a special meaning? If so, what is the history of your name? Do you like your name? Why or why not?

- In our story, God revealed Himself to Abram as "El Shaddai," meaning "God Almighty." Why do you think God revealed Himself by this new name (v. 1)? How is this name related to God's promise and Abram and Sarai's age?

- What did God say to Abram and why do you think He changed his name (v. 2-5)? What does "Abraham" mean? How long did God say His covenant with Abraham would last and how long did He say that his offspring would possess the land of Canaan (v. 6-8)? What is significant about this for us today?

- What did God instruct Abraham to do as a sign of His covenant between them (v. 9-14)? Why do you think God chose circumcision as the sign of the covenant? In what ways can circumcision be compared to baptism today?

- Why do you think God changed Sarai's name (v. 15-16)? What does "Sarah" mean? What promises did God make concerning Sarah? Why do you think Abraham "laughed" (v. 17)? Why is this an *attitude to change*?

- What was Abraham's prayer request concerning his son Ishmael (v. 18-19)? Why do you think God answered "no" to this request? In what ways was Abraham's prayer request an attempt to settle for less than the best?

- What did God promise concerning Ishmael (v. 20)? What nation came from Ishmael? What is significant about this for us today?

- Why should you never want to settle for second best from God? Can you give a testimony of a time when God answered "no" to your prayer and it was for your best? What things are required of you to receive God's best?

PRAYER:

Let's pray for one another to be willing to wait with faith for God's best.

PRAYER REQUESTS:

BI-MONTHLY MISSION PROJECT NOTES:

WEEK 4

Weekly Bible Reading: .... Stories from Genesis
Weekly Bible Study: .... Genesis 22:1-14

GENESIS 18:1-33   [CIRCLE ONE: S P A C E]
Personal Study Notes: _____
_____
_____
_____

GENESIS 19:1-38   [CIRCLE ONE: S P A C E]
Personal Study Notes: _____
_____
_____
_____

GENESIS 20-1-18   [CIRCLE ONE: S P A C E]
Personal Study Notes: _____
_____
_____
_____

GENESIS 21:1-34   [CIRCLE ONE: S P A C E]
Personal Study Notes: _____
_____
_____
_____

GENESIS 22:1-24   [CIRCLE ONE: S P A C E]
Personal Study Notes: _____
_____
_____
_____

Read carefully one chapter of the Bible five days a week. In each chapter look for a . . .
Sin to Confess / **P**romise to Claim / **A**ttitude to Change / **C**ommand to Obey / **E**xample to Follow.

THE SACRIFICE OF ISAAC
(GENESIS 22:1-14)

WEEKLY ASSIGNMENTS:

Lead Prayer Time: _____

Tell the Story (Paraphrase): _____

Read the Text: _____

Facilitate Bible Study: _____

DISCUSSION QUESTIONS:

- What is the hardest test you have ever taken? Did you pass or fail? How do you feel when you pass a difficult test? How do you feel when you fail one?

- In this story, God tested Abraham. Why do you think God tested Abraham (v. 1)? Do you think God still tests His people today? Why or why not? Read James 1:2-4. When God "tests" us, what is His purpose?

- How did God test Abraham and why was this a very difficult test (v. 2)? Besides being Abraham's only son, what else was special about Isaac?

- How did Abraham respond to this test (v. 3)? Why do you think Abraham was able to respond as he did? How do you think you would have responded? On Abraham's three-day journey to Mt. Moriah, what do you think was going through his mind (v. 4)?

- Upon arriving at Mt. Moriah, what two bold statements of faith did Abraham make (v. 5-8)? As *an example to follow*, why is it important for us to speak out and declare our faith in times of testing?

- Read Jn. 1:29. How was Abraham's second statement of faith also a great word of prophesy about the coming Messiah (v. 8)? How many comparisons can you make between Isaac and Jesus?

- At what point did God rescue Abraham from this trial (v. 9-11)? What did God say that He learned about Abraham from this trial (v. 12)? In what ways do the trials of life help our faith to grow?

- Abraham named this place, "Jehovah-Jireh," meaning, "the Lord will provide" (v. 13-14)? What did God provide in place of Isaac? What has God provided for us so that we might be saved?

- Can you give a testimony of how Jehovah-Jireh provided for you in a time of trial or testing? Do you need prayer today for a trial in your life?

PRAYER:

Let's pray for one another to trust Jehovah-Jireh in our times of trial.

PRAYER REQUESTS:

BI-MONTHLY MISSION PROJECT NOTES:

WEEK

Weekly Bible Reading: .... Stories from Genesis
Weekly Bible Study: .... Genesis 25:19-34

GENESIS 24:1-28   [CIRCLE ONE: S P A C E]
Personal Study Notes: _____
_____
_____
_____

GENESIS 24:29-67   [CIRCLE ONE: S P A C E]
Personal Study Notes: _____
_____
_____
_____

GENESIS 25:19-34   [CIRCLE ONE: S P A C E]
Personal Study Notes: _____
_____
_____
_____

GENESIS 26:1-35   [CIRCLE ONE: S P A C E]
Personal Study Notes: _____
_____
_____
_____

GENESIS 27:1-46   [CIRCLE ONE: S P A C E]
Personal Study Notes: _____
_____
_____
_____

Read carefully one chapter of the Bible five days a week. In each chapter look for a . . .
Sin to Confess / **P**romise to Claim / **A**ttitude to Change / **C**ommand to Obey / **E**xample to Follow.

ESAU SELLS HIS BIRTHRIGHT
(GENESIS 25:19-34)

WEEKLY ASSIGNMENTS:

Lead Prayer Time: _____

Tell the Story (Paraphrase): _____

Read the Text: _____

Facilitate Bible Study: _____

DISCUSSION QUESTIONS:

- How many siblings do you have? Have you and your siblings ever had any rivalries between you? What did you most often fight over?

- In our story, we are told of the rivalry between Isaac's two sons, Jacob and Esau. When Isaac's wife, Rebekah, was barren, what important thing did he do for her (v. 19-21)? What did God do in response? Why is it important for husbands and wives to pray for one another?

- When Rebekah was troubled about the condition of her pregnancy, what important thing did she do (v. 22)? What did the Lord reveal to her (v. 23)? Why is it important for us to pray when we are troubled and need guidance?

- After Rebekah gave birth to twins, what physical traits are we told about her first-born son Esau (v. 24-25)? What are we told about Jacob (v. 26)? Why did Isaac favor Esau?

Why did Rebekah favor Jacob (v. 27-28)? Why is parental favoritism detrimental to any family? How can you avoid this?

- In these days, what was a "birthright" and why was it important (v. 29-30)? What did the birthright mean for Esau? Why do you think Jacob wanted it?

- What foolish decision did Esau make and why (v. 32-33)? Why do you think the Bible says, "Esau despised his birthright" (v. 34)?

- *As a sin to confess*, why is it wrong for you to take advantage of a brother or sister for personal gain? Likewise, why is it foolish and irresponsible for you to trade something of lasting value for temporary pleasure?

- What are the things in your life today that are truly valuable? Who is the ultimate source of these blessings? In what ways are you grateful, respectful, and responsible for the things of great value in your life?

PRAYER:

Let's pray today and give thanks to God for the things that are truly valuable to us and pray that we will take great responsibility for how we treat them.

PRAYER REQUESTS:

BI-MONTHLY MISSION PROJECT NOTES:

WEEK 6

Weekly Bible Reading: .... Stories from Genesis
Weekly Bible Study: .... Genesis 32:22-32

GENESIS 28:1-22   [CIRCLE ONE: S P A C E]

Personal Study Notes: _____

_____

_____

_____

GENESIS 29:1-35   [CIRCLE ONE: S P A C E]

Personal Study Notes: _____

_____

_____

_____

GENESIS 30:1-24   [CIRCLE ONE: S P A C E]

Personal Study Notes: _____

_____

_____

_____

GENESIS 32:1-32   [CIRCLE ONE: S P A C E]

Personal Study Notes: _____

_____

_____

_____

GENESIS 33:1-20   [CIRCLE ONE: S P A C E]

Personal Study Notes: _____

_____

_____

_____

Read carefully one chapter of the Bible five days a week. In each chapter look for a . . .
Sin to Confess / **P**romise to Claim / **A**ttitude to Change / **C**ommand to Obey / **E**xample to Follow.

JACOB WRESTLES WITH GOD
(GENESIS 32:22-32)

WEEKLY ASSIGNMENTS:

Lead Prayer Time: _____

Tell the Story (Paraphrase): _____

Read the Text: _____

Facilitate Bible Study: _____

DISCUSSION QUESTIONS:

- In a metaphorical sense, do you ever wrestle with God? When is the last time that you wrestled with God over something and how did it go for you?

- In our story, Jacob wrestled with God all night. Do you think the man who wrestled all night with Jacob was possibly a preincarnate appearance of Jesus Christ (v. 22-24)? Why or why not?

- Up to this point, in what ways had Jacob been wrestling with God in his life? When a person wrestles with God, why does God sometimes let him or her win? Could God always win if He wanted to? Why or why not?

- When the man who wrestled with Jacob did not prevail, why do you think He dislocated Jacob's hip (v. 25)? Read Hebrews 12:5-6, 11. God's discipline may be painful, but why is it sometimes necessary in a person's life?

- After the man dislocated his hip, why do you think He continued to let Jacob hold on to Him (v. 26a)? In what way is this *an example for us to follow*?

- What did Jacob request of this man in order for him to let Him go (v. 26b)? Do you think the man was pleased with Jacob's request? Why or why not? What was the man's response to Jacob (v. 27-28)? Why do you think He changed Jacob's name to Israel?

- In what way had Jacob "striven with God...and prevailed" (v. 29)? Read Ex. 33:20. If no man can see the face of God and live, why do you think Jacob was able to wrestle with God and survive (v. 30)?

- Is there a time in your life when God disciplined you out of His love for you? Can you share about this?

- Have you ever "wrestled with God" in prayer and refused to let go of Him until He answered your request? Can you share about this?

PRAYER:

Let's pray for one another to have the faith and courage to hold on to God in prayer until our prayers are answered.

PRAYER REQUESTS:

BI-MONTHLY MISSION PROJECT NOTES:

WEEK 7

Weekly Bible Reading: . . . . Stories from Genesis
Weekly Bible Study: . . . . Genesis 39:1-23

GENESIS 34:1-31   [CIRCLE ONE: S P A C E]
Personal Study Notes: _____
_____
_____
_____

GENESIS 35:1-29   [CIRCLE ONE: S P A C E]
Personal Study Notes: _____
_____
_____
_____

GENESIS 37:1-36   [CIRCLE ONE: S P A C E]
Personal Study Notes: _____
_____
_____
_____

GENESIS 38:1-30   [CIRCLE ONE: S P A C E]
Personal Study Notes: _____
_____
_____
_____

GENESIS 39:1-23   [CIRCLE ONE: S P A C E]
Personal Study Notes: _____
_____
_____
_____

Read carefully one chapter of the Bible five days a week. In each chapter look for a . . .
Sin to Confess / **P**romise to Claim / **A**ttitude to Change / **C**ommand to Obey / **E**xample to Follow.

JOSEPH AND POTIPHAR'S WIFE
(GENESIS 39:1-23)

WEEKLY ASSIGNMENTS:

Lead Prayer Time: _____

Tell the Story (Paraphrase): _____

Read the Text: _____

Facilitate Bible Study: _____

DISCUSSION QUESTIONS:

- Throughout history, in what ways has sexual temptation destroyed many lives? What are some common sexual sins that people fall into today?

- In our story, Joseph was sold as a slave to Potiphar, an Egyptian officer. Even in his great affliction, who was "with Joseph" (v. 1-2a)? What series of good things happened in Joseph's life because "the Lord was with him" (v. 2b-6)?

- When we walk close with the Lord, why must we watch out for Satan? In what way did Satan, come after Joseph (v. 7)?

- How did Joseph respond to the seductive invitation of Potiphar's wife (v. 7-9)? What truth did Joseph realize about sexual sin that many do not seem to realize today (v. 9b)? Why do you think Satan kept coming back with this same temptation "day after day" (v. 10)?

- What did Potiphar's wife do on her final attempt to seduce Joseph (v. 11-12)? In what ways does Joseph give us *an example to follow* when facing sexual temptation? Read 2 Tim. 2:22. Why must we flee or run from sexual sins?

- What false accusation did Potiphar's wife make against Joseph (v. 13-18)? What damage did this do to Joseph (v. 19-20)? How does it make you feel to be falsely accused? How can we guard ourselves against false accusations?

- Even in prison, who was "with Joseph" (v. 21)? What series of good things began to happen because "the Lord was with Joseph" in prison (v. 21-23)? Why is it important for us to do right even when we suffer wrong?

- What important lessons can we learn from Joseph about battling sexual temptation? Why must we not give in to sexual temptation? Even in the worst of times, what can we learn from Joseph about trusting in the Lord?

PRAYER:

Let's pray today for wisdom and strength to walk close with the Lord and to flee from all sexual temptations.

PRAYER REQUESTS:

BI-MONTHLY MISSION PROJECT NOTES:

WEEK

GENESIS 40:1-23   [CIRCLE ONE: S P A C E]

Personal Study Notes: _____

_____

_____

_____

GENESIS 41:1-36   [CIRCLE ONE: S P A C E]

Personal Study Notes: _____

_____

_____

_____

GENESIS 41:37-57   [CIRCLE ONE: S P A C E]

Personal Study Notes: _____

_____

_____

_____

GENESIS 42:1-38   [CIRCLE ONE: S P A C E]

Personal Study Notes: _____

_____

_____

_____

GENESIS 43:1-34   [CIRCLE ONE: S P A C E]

Personal Study Notes: _____

_____

_____

_____

Read carefully one chapter of the Bible five days a week. In each chapter look for a . . .
Sin to Confess / **P**romise to Claim / **A**ttitude to Change / **C**ommand to Obey / **E**xample to Follow.

JOSEPH IS EXALTED
(GENESIS 41:37-57)

WEEKLY ASSIGNMENTS:

Lead Prayer Time: _____

Tell the Story (Paraphrase): _____

Read the Text: _____

Facilitate Bible Study: _____

DISCUSSION QUESTIONS:

- Hard knocks are a part of life. How can the hard knocks of life help us to become better people? How can our faith help us endure hard knocks?

- In our story, Joseph was finally exalted after many years of hard knocks and setbacks. What was it about Joseph that led Pharaoh to promote him to second in command in Egypt (v. 37-38)?

- For many years Joseph endured numerous trials, but what resulted in him being exalted (v. 39-41)? Read 1 Pet. 5:6. In what ways was Joseph's life a testimony to this promise?

- What series of actions did Pharaoh take to demonstrate Joseph's new and exalted position over Egypt (v. 42-45)? After all Joseph had been through, how do you think this made him feel?

- God gave Joseph a fourteen-year economic plan as leader over Egypt. What wise principles were included in this plan (v. 46-48)? How successful was this plan? In what ways was Joseph's faith related to this plan (v. 49)?

- What did Joseph name his first-born son (v. 50-51)? What did his name mean and how does it relate to Joseph's life? What did he name his second son (v. 52)? What does his name mean and how does it relate to Joseph's life?

- God had great plans for Joseph and his life made a big difference (v. 53-57). How might Joseph's life have been different if he had become bitter and angry with God? As an example to follow, what can we learn from Joseph about humble and persevering faith in God?

- Can you share a testimony about a time in your life when you humbled yourself under the mighty hand of God and He exalted you in due time?

PRAYER:

Let's pray today that God will give each of us a humble and persevering faith in the midst of our trials.

PRAYER REQUESTS:

BI-MONTHLY MISSION PROJECT NOTES:

WEEK 9

GENESIS 44:1-34
[CIRCLE ONE: S P A C E]

Personal Study Notes: _____
_____
_____
_____

GENESIS 45:1-28
[CIRCLE ONE: S P A C E]

Personal Study Notes: _____
_____
_____
_____

GENESIS 47:1-31
[CIRCLE ONE: S P A C E]

Personal Study Notes: _____
_____
_____
_____

GENESIS 48:1-22
[CIRCLE ONE: S P A C E]

Personal Study Notes: _____
_____
_____
_____

GENESIS 50:1-26
[CIRCLE ONE: S P A C E]

Personal Study Notes: _____
_____
_____
_____

Read carefully one chapter of the Bible five days a week. In each chapter look for a . . .
Sin to Confess / **P**romise to Claim / **A**ttitude to Change / **C**ommand to Obey / **E**xample to Follow.

JOSEPH'S FAITH IN GOD'S SOVEREIGNTY
(GENESIS 50:15-26)

WEEKLY ASSIGNMENTS:

Lead Prayer Time: _____

Tell the Story (Paraphrase): _____

Read the Text: _____

Facilitate Bible Study: _____

DISCUSSION QUESTIONS:

- It is often said, "Revenge is sweet." What is it about human nature that causes people to seek after revenge? Is revenge really sweet?

- In our story, Joseph has been miraculously reunited with his family. After their father had died, what fears did Joseph's brothers have concerning their relationship with Joseph (v. 15)? In what ways do our evil deeds seem to come back and haunt us?

- How did Joseph's brothers respond to their fears (v. 16-18)? How did Joseph respond to their fears (v. 19-21)? What did Joseph mean by asking, "Am I in the place of God" (v. 19)? How did Joseph's faith in God's sovereignty help him overcome feelings of resentment and thoughts of revenge?

- Read Romans 8:28. How does this verse relate to Joseph's understanding of his situation (v. 20)? In what ways did God cause the evil done to Joseph to work out for his good? As an *attitude to change*, how can your personal faith in God's sovereignty help you endure times of evil and suffering?

- How long did Joseph live and why was this a blessing (v. 22-23)? What promise did God reveal to Joseph about his family before he died (v. 24)? Why do you think God revealed to Joseph things He didn't reveal to others?

- Why do you think Joseph made his brothers promise they would carry his bones out of Egypt and back to the land of promise (v. 25-26)? What does this promise reveal about Joseph's faith?

- The next time you experience evil and suffering, what lessons can you draw from Joseph's testimony? How can your faith in God's sovereign ways help you to be more forgiving and compassionate to those who hurt you?

PRAYER:

Let's pray today that God will give us the faith to believe that all things work together for good for those who love God and are called according to His purposes.

PRAYER REQUESTS:

BI-MONTHLY MISSION PROJECT NOTES:

WEEK 10

EXODUS 1:1-22
[CIRCLE ONE: S P A C E]

*Personal Study Notes:*_____

_____

_____

_____

EXODUS 2:1-25
[CIRCLE ONE: S P A C E]

*Personal Study Notes:*_____

_____

_____

_____

EXODUS 3:1-22
[CIRCLE ONE: S P A C E]

*Personal Study Notes:*_____

_____

_____

_____

EXODUS 4:1-31
[CIRCLE ONE: S P A C E]

*Personal Study Notes:*_____

_____

_____

_____

EXODUS 5:1-23
[CIRCLE ONE: S P A C E]

*Personal Study Notes:*_____

_____

_____

_____

Read carefully one chapter of the Bible five days a week. In each chapter look for a . . .
Sin to Confess / **P**romise to Claim / **A**ttitude to Change / **C**ommand to Obey / **E**xample to Follow.

MOSES AND THE BURNING BUSH
(EXODUS 3:1-22)

WEEKLY ASSIGNMENTS:

Lead Prayer Time: _____

Tell the Story (Paraphrase): _____

Read the Text: _____

Facilitate Bible Study: _____

DISCUSSION QUESTIONS:

- What is the strangest thing you have ever seen? What thoughts or feelings did you have when you saw this?

- In our story, Moses saw a burning bush that would not burn up. Where was Moses when he saw the burning bush and what was he doing (v. 1-2)? What do you think his thoughts and feelings might have been when he saw this?

- Why do you think Moses turned aside to see this great sight (v. 3)? When God spoke from the bush, what initial instructions did He give Moses (v. 4-5)? How should God's people respond when they are on holy ground?

- Who did God tell Moses that He was (v. 6)? Who were Abraham, Isaac, and Jacob, and why do you think God introduced Himself as their God? What did God tell Moses that He had seen and heard about His people in Egypt (v. 7)? What did God tell Moses that He had come down to do (v. 8-9)?

- If God had come down to save His people from Egypt, why was it necessary to send Moses (v. 10)? When God is at work around us, why does He always call His people to join Him in that work? What happens when we do?

- What was Moses' initial response to God's call (v. 11)? How did God respond to his excuse (v. 12)? Why does God call His people to do things we can never do without Him? When God says, "I will be with you," what does He mean? As a *sin to confess*, why does making excuses to God show a lack of faith?

- What did God tell Moses that His name was (v. 13-14)? What does it mean that God's name is "I AM?" What did "I AM" say He would do for His people (v. 15-17)? What did He say He would do to the Egyptians (v. 18-22)?

- Can you share about a time when God called you to do something you could never do without Him? What is He leading you to do now that requires faith?

PRAYER:

Let's pray today that we will have the faith and courage to follow God's call.

PRAYER REQUESTS:

BI-MONTHLY MISSION PROJECT NOTES:

WEEK  11

Weekly Bible Reading: . . . . Stories from Exodus
Weekly Bible Study: . . . . Exodus 12:1-14

EXODUS 7:1-25
[CIRCLE ONE: S P A C E]

Personal Study Notes: _____

_____

_____

_____

EXODUS 8:1-32
[CIRCLE ONE: S P A C E]

Personal Study Notes: _____

_____

_____

_____

EXODUS 9:1-35
[CIRCLE ONE: S P A C E]

Personal Study Notes: _____

_____

_____

_____

EXODUS 10:1-29
[CIRCLE ONE: S P A C E]

Personal Study Notes: _____

_____

_____

_____

EXODUS 12:1-32
[CIRCLE ONE: S P A C E]

Personal Study Notes: _____

_____

_____

_____

Read carefully one chapter of the Bible five days a week. In each chapter look for a . . .
Sin to Confess / **P**romise to Claim / **A**ttitude to Change / **C**ommand to Obey / **E**xample to Follow.

THE PASSOVER LAMB
(EXODUS 12:1-14)

WEEKLY ASSIGNMENTS:

Lead Prayer Time: _____

Tell the Story (Paraphrase): _____

Read the Text: _____

Facilitate Bible Study: _____

DISCUSSION QUESTIONS:

- Do you like to follow instructions and why? When is it important to do so?

- In our story, God instructed the Israelites to prepare for the Passover before His final plague on the Egyptians. What clear instructions did God give about the Passover lamb (v. 1-7)? Why was it important for the lamb to be "without blemish" (v. 5)? What were they to do with the blood of the lamb (v. 7)?

- Read John 1:28-29. How is John the Baptist's description of Jesus related to the Passover Lamb? Why was it necessary for Jesus to be "without blemish?"

- What were the Israelites instructed to eat for the Passover meal (v. 8-10)? What do you think is the significance of "unleavened bread" and "bitter herbs?" In what manner were the Israelites to eat the Passover meal (v. 11)? Why do you think they were instructed to eat it in haste?

- What did God say He would do throughout the land of Egypt on the night of Passover (v. 12)? What did God promise to do when He saw the blood of the Lamb over the door of a household (v. 13)?

- Read Heb. 11:28. How was faith involved in the salvation of the Israelites during the Passover? If the blood of the Lamb was not over the door of a household, do you think they would have been saved? Why or why not?

- How long did God command the Israelites to keep the feast of Passover (v. 14)? Why do you think God wanted the Israelites to keep the Passover meal from generation to generation? How important is it for us today to pass on the message of salvation by faith in Christ from generation to generation?

- As *an example to follow*, how could you use the story of Passover to witness to others today about their need for faith in Jesus Christ?

PRAYER:

Let's pray today for God to open the eyes of the lost to see the true Lamb of God and for God to give us opportunities to witness to them.

PRAYER REQUESTS:

BI-MONTHLY MISSION PROJECT NOTES:

WEEK 12

EXODUS 12:33-51
[CIRCLE ONE: S P A C E]

*Personal Study Notes:*_____

_____

_____

_____

EXODUS 14:1-31
[CIRCLE ONE: S P A C E]

*Personal Study Notes:*_____

_____

_____

_____

_____

EXODUS 15:1-27
[CIRCLE ONE: S P A C E]

*Personal Study Notes:*_____

_____

_____

_____

_____

EXODUS 16:1-36
[CIRCLE ONE: S P A C E]

*Personal Study Notes:*_____

_____

_____

_____

_____

EXODUS 17:1-16
[CIRCLE ONE: S P A C E]

*Personal Study Notes:*_____

_____

_____

_____

_____

Read carefully one chapter of the Bible five days a week. In each chapter look for a . . .
Sin to Confess / **P**romise to Claim / **A**ttitude to Change / **C**ommand to Obey / **E**xample to Follow.

THE PARTING OF THE RED SEA
(EXODUS 14:1-18)

WEEKLY ASSIGNMENTS:

Lead Prayer Time: _____

Tell the Story (Paraphrase): _____

Read the Text: _____

Facilitate Bible Study: _____

DISCUSSION QUESTIONS:

• When is the last time you were in a situation where there seemed to be no way out? How did you respond?

• In our story, God parted the Red Sea to save the Israelites from the Egyptians. Why do you think God continued to harden Pharaoh's heart (v. 1-4a)? What did the Lord want the Egyptians to know beyond doubt (v. 4b)?

• When the Israelites saw Pharaoh and his army coming after them, how did they respond (v. 10)? What accusation did they make against Moses (v. 11-12)? Why do you think they responded in this way?

• What word of faith and encouragement did Moses speak to the people (v. 13-14)? How had Moses' faith grown from the time when the Lord first called Him to go speak to Pharaoh?

- What did the Lord instruct Moses to do in order for the Israelites to be saved from Pharaoh's army (v. 15-16)? What did God say He was going to do to Pharaoh's army (v. 17)? Read Heb. 11:29. What part did faith play in this?

- Why do you think some people question the validity of this great miracle? What is God teaching His people by performing such a great miracle? Why do you think God allows His people to be in situations where there seems to be no way out? What part does our faith play in this?

- What did the Egyptians learn about the God of the Israelites from this incident (v. 18)? Read Exo. 15:2, 6, 11, 13, 18. What did Moses and the Israelites learn about their God from this incident?

- As *an attitude to change*, how should you respond when you find yourself in a situation where there seems to be no way out? Can someone share a testimony of God's faithfulness in a time such as this?

PRAYER:

Let's pray today for faith and trust in God when we face difficult situations.

PRAYER REQUESTS:

BI-MONTHLY MISSION PROJECT NOTES:

WEEK 13

Weekly Bible Reading: .... Stories from Exodus
Weekly Bible Study: .... Exodus 20:1-21

EXODUS 18:1-27
[CIRCLE ONE: S P A C E]

*Personal Study Notes:*_____
_____
_____
_____

EXODUS 19:1-25
[CIRCLE ONE: S P A C E]

*Personal Study Notes:*_____
_____
_____
_____

EXODUS 20:1-26
[CIRCLE ONE: S P A C E]

*Personal Study Notes:*_____
_____
_____
_____

EXODUS 24:1-18
[CIRCLE ONE: S P A C E]

*Personal Study Notes:*_____
_____
_____
_____

EXODUS 31:1-18
[CIRCLE ONE: S P A C E]

*Personal Study Notes:*_____
_____
_____
_____

Read carefully one chapter of the Bible five days a week. In each chapter look for a . . .
Sin to Confess / **P**romise to Claim / **A**ttitude to Change / **C**ommand to Obey / **E**xample to Follow.

THE TEN COMMANDMENTS
(EXODUS 20:1-21)

WEEKLY ASSIGNMENTS:

Lead Prayer Time: _____

Tell the Story (Paraphrase): _____

Read the Text: _____

Facilitate Bible Study: _____

DISCUSSION QUESTIONS:

- Are you a rule follower or a rule breaker? What makes you this way?

- In our story, God gave Moses the Ten Commandments. When God spoke to Moses on Mount Sinai, what did He remind Moses that He had done for him and the Israelites (v. 1-2)? Why do you think God reminded Moses of this before giving him the Ten Commandments?

- What is the first commandment and why is it of supreme importance (v. 3)? Why did God not want His people to make any carved images (v. 4-6)? What did God say would happen to those who worship carved images and what did He mean by this? How is idolatry passed from one generation to the next?

- What did God say He would show to those who love Him and keep His commandments? Read John 14:15. How are love and obedience related?

- Why is it important to honor the name of the Lord (v. 7)? What does it mean to take His name in vain? What is revealed about a person who does this?

- What day of the week is the Sabbath and what did God say about the Sabbath (v. 8-11)? Read Acts 20:7 & 1 Cor. 16:2. What day is the "first day of the week?" Why do you think the early church began to worship on Sunday?

- How do you show honor to your father and mother? Why is this important and what *promise to claim* is attached to honoring your parents (v. 12)?

- What is different about murder, adultery, stealing, lying, and coveting that make them sins against God and man (v. 13-16)? Is it a sin to take the life of an unborn child? Is it a sin to lust over sexual images? Why or why not?

- Why did God allow the people to see the thunder and lighting on the mountain (v. 18-21)? Why is it good to have a healthy fear of God? What commandments do you most struggle with? How can your D-Group help?

PRAYER:

Let's pray today for God to give each of us a healthy fear of Him.

PRAYER REQUESTS:

BI-MONTHLY MISSION PROJECT NOTES:

WEEK  14

Weekly Bible Reading: . . . . Stories from Exodus
Weekly Bible Study: . . . . Exodus 35:4-35

EXODUS 32:1-35　　　　　[CIRCLE ONE: S P A C E]

Personal Study Notes: _____

_____

_____

_____

EXODUS 33:1-23　　　　　[CIRCLE ONE: S P A C E]

Personal Study Notes: _____

_____

_____

_____

EXODUS 34:1-35　　　　　[CIRCLE ONE: S P A C E]

Personal Study Notes: _____

_____

_____

_____

EXODUS 35:1-35　　　　　[CIRCLE ONE: S P A C E]

Personal Study Notes: _____

_____

_____

_____

EXODUS 40:1-38　　　　　[CIRCLE ONE: S P A C E]

Personal Study Notes: _____

_____

_____

_____

Read carefully one chapter of the Bible five days a week. In each chapter look for a . . .
Sin to Confess / **P**romise to Claim / **A**ttitude to Change / **C**ommand to Obey / **E**xample to Follow.

GIVING FOR THE TABERNACLE
(EXODUS 35:4-35)

WEEKLY ASSIGNMENTS:

Lead Prayer Time: _____

Tell the Story (Paraphrase): _____

Read the Text: _____

Facilitate Bible Study: _____

DISCUSSION QUESTIONS:

- How do you feel about giving tithes and offerings to the Lord? Why do you think the subject offends some people?

- In our story, God instructed the people of Israel to give an offering for the building of the Tabernacle. Why do you think God wanted the people to give for this instead of providing everything Himself (v. 4-5a)?

- God wanted the people to give with a "generous heart" (v. 5). What does it mean to have a generous heart? Why is it important to God for His people to have a generous heart?

- What kinds of things were the people instructed to give (v. 5b-9)? What were the skilled craftsmen instructed to do (v. 10)? What different kinds of skilled people were involved in the construction of the tabernacle (v. 11-19)?

- How did the people respond (v. 20-29)? What do the phrases "heart stirred," spirit moved," and "willing heart," say about the attitude of the people toward giving? This offering is called a "freewill offering" (v. 29)? What is a "freewill offering?" How is a freewill offering different from the tithe?

- Who were Bazalel and Oholiab and what kind of spiritual gifts had God given them (v. 30-35)? How were they to use their spiritual gifts? Who is someone you know today who is gifted like Bazalel and Oholiab?

- Read Exodus 36:2-7. How much did the people give for the tabernacle? What were the people commanded to do in these verses? In this instance, how are the people of Israel an *example for us* to follow?

- Would you consider yourself as a person with a generous heart? Why or why not? Why is it important for us to give both tithes and offerings to God?

PRAYER:

Let's pray today for God to give each of us a more generous heart.

PRAYER REQUESTS:

BI-MONTHLY MISSION PROJECT NOTES:

WEEK

Weekly Bible Reading: . . . . Stories from Leviticus

Weekly Bible Study: . . . . Leviticus 10:1-11

LEVITICUS 9:1-24   [CIRCLE ONE: S P A C E]

Personal Study Notes: _____

_____

_____

_____

LEVITICUS 10:1-20   [CIRCLE ONE: S P A C E]

Personal Study Notes: _____

_____

_____

_____

LEVITICUS 16:1-34   [CIRCLE ONE: S P A C E]

Personal Study Notes: _____

_____

_____

_____

LEVITICUS 23:1-44   [CIRCLE ONE: S P A C E]

Personal Study Notes: _____

_____

_____

_____

LEVITICUS 26:1-46   [CIRCLE ONE: S P A C E]

Personal Study Notes: _____

_____

_____

_____

Read carefully one chapter of the Bible five days a week. In each chapter look for a . . .
Sin to Confess / **P**romise to Claim / **A**ttitude to Change / **C**ommand to Obey / **E**xample to Follow.

THE HOLY AND THE COMMON
(LEVITICUS 10:1-11)

WEEKLY ASSIGNMENTS:

Lead Prayer Time: _____

Tell the Story (Paraphrase): _____

Read the Text: _____

Facilitate Bible Study: _____

DISCUSSION QUESTIONS:

- What is the difference between something that is holy and something that is common? Why is it important to distinguish between the two?

- In our story, two priests made the mistake of treating as common something that was holy. Who were Nadab and Abihu and what special privileges had God given them (v. 1)? What responsibilities come with special privileges?

- What sin did Nadab and Abihu commit before the Lord (v. 1)? What do you think "unauthorized" or "strange" fire means? What happened to these two sons of Aaron (v. 2)? Why do you think the Lord did this?

- What did Moses say to Aaron right after the death of his sons (v. 3)? What do you think is the meaning of God's words to Aaron? Why do you think Aaron held his peace?

- What specific command did the Lord give to Aaron after his sons were taken away (v. 8-10)? What does this imply about the deaths of Nadab and Abihu? How does strong drink impair our judgments and lead to bad choices? Can you think of other examples of this in the Scriptures and in real life today?

- What does it mean to distinguish between the holy and the common and between the unclean and the clean (v. 10)? In what ways had Nadab and Abihu violated this principle? Why is this *an important command to obey*?

- Can you think of some examples today where people fail to distinguish between the holy and the common? What are the potential consequences of violating this failure?

- What actions can you take that will help you distinguish between the holy and the common? In what ways can you help others with this?

PRAYER:

Let's pray today for God to give us wisdom to distinguish between the holy and the common.

PRAYER REQUESTS:

BI-MONTHLY MISSION PROJECT NOTES:

WEEK 16

Weekly Bible Reading: .... Stories from Leviticus
Weekly Bible Study: .... Numbers 13:1-33

NUMBERS 11:1-35   [CIRCLE ONE: S P A C E]
*Personal Study Notes:*_____

_____

_____

_____

NUMBERS 12:1-16   [CIRCLE ONE: S P A C E]
*Personal Study Notes:*_____

_____

_____

_____

NUMBERS 13:1-33   [CIRCLE ONE: S P A C E]
*Personal Study Notes:*_____

_____

_____

_____

NUMBERS 14:1-45   [CIRCLE ONE: S P A C E]
*Personal Study Notes:*_____

_____

_____

_____

NUMBERS 16:1-50   [CIRCLE ONE: S P A C E]
*Personal Study Notes:*_____

_____

_____

_____

Read carefully one chapter of the Bible five days a week. In each chapter look for a . . .
Sin to Confess / **P**romise to Claim / **A**ttitude to Change / **C**ommand to Obey / **E**xample to Follow.

THE REPORT OF THE TWELVE SPIES
(NUMBERS 13:1-33)

WEEKLY ASSIGNMENTS:

Lead Prayer Time: _____

Tell the Story (Paraphrase): _____

Read the Text: _____

Facilitate Bible Study: _____

DISCUSSION QUESTIONS:

- When was the last time you found yourself at odds with the majority? How did you respond to this and how did it make you feel?

- In our story, Moses sent twelve spies into the land of Canaan. Who were these men and what was their purpose (v. 1-24)?

- After they returned, what positive report did the twelve spies give about the land (v. 25-27)? What negative report did they give (v. 28-29)?

- Which spy found himself at odds with the majority (v. 30a)? What did Caleb say to the people and what does this tell us about him (v. 30b)?

- How did the majority respond to Caleb's words and what does this tell us about them (v. 31)? What did they not learn from Egypt about their God?

- The Bible says, "they brought to the people of Israel a bad report" (v. 32-33). In what ways does Satan use a "bad report" in the lives of God's people? What were the consequences of the spies' "bad report?"

- Read Numbers 14:5-10. What one other spy agreed with Caleb? What did Joshua and Caleb say to the people and how did the people respond? What stopped the people of Israel from stoning Joshua and Caleb?

- Read Numbers 14:36-38. What happened to the spies who gave the bad report? How did God reward Joshua and Caleb? What kind of spy do you think you would have been and why?

- In the church today, do you think people are more likely to listen to negative or positive reports and why? When you face challenges and negativity, why is the faith and courage of Joshua and Caleb *an example to follow*?

PRAYER:

Let's pray today that God will give us the faith and courage of Joshua and Caleb and that we will not join in with those who give negative reports.

PRAYER REQUESTS:

BI-MONTHLY MISSION PROJECT NOTES:

WEEK 17

Weekly Bible Reading: .... Stories from Numbers
Weekly Bible Study: .... Numbers 21:4-9

NUMBERS 17:1-13
[CIRCLE ONE: S P A C E]

*Personal Study Notes:*_____

_____

_____

_____

NUMBERS 20:1-29
[CIRCLE ONE: S P A C E]

*Personal Study Notes:*_____

_____

_____

_____

NUMBERS 21:1-35
[CIRCLE ONE: S P A C E]

*Personal Study Notes:*_____

_____

_____

_____

NUMBERS 22:1-41
[CIRCLE ONE: S P A C E]

*Personal Study Notes:*_____

_____

_____

_____

NUMBERS 27:1-23
[CIRCLE ONE: S P A C E]

*Personal Study Notes:*_____

_____

_____

_____

Read carefully one chapter of the Bible five days a week. In each chapter look for a . . .
Sin to Confess / **P**romise to Claim / **A**ttitude to Change / **C**ommand to Obey / **E**xample to Follow.

THE BRONZE SERPENT IN THE WILDERNESS
(NUMBERS 21:4-9)

WEEKLY ASSIGNMENTS:

Lead Prayer Time: _____

Tell the Story (Paraphrase): _____

Read the Text: _____

Facilitate Bible Study: _____

DISCUSSION QUESTIONS:

- What is the closest encounter you have had with a snake? How do you feel about snakes?

- In our story, the Israelites become impatient with God and Moses. Why did they become impatient and what complaints did they raise (v. 4-5)? Were their complaints justified? Why or why not?

- How did the Lord respond to the people's impatience and complaints (v. 6)? What can we learn about God from this instance? As an *attitude to change*, why is it important to have a healthy fear of God?

- How did the people respond to God's discipline and judgment on their sin (v. 7a)? Read Heb. 12:5-6, 11. God's discipline is never pleasant, but why is it profitable? How was God's discipline "profitable" in this instance?

- In response to the people's repentance, what did Moses do for them (v. 7b)? In answer to His prayer, what did God instruct Moses to do (v. 8a)? In order to live, what must the people do and how did this require their faith (v. 8b)?

- Read John 3:13-16. What did Jesus say about this story? In what ways was "the serpent lifted up in the wilderness" a foreshadowing of Christ? What parallels can be made between Christ and the bronze serpent?

- How is John 3:16 and Num. 21:8 related? How could you use this Old Testament story to share the gospel with someone today?

- Throughout the Bible, the message of the gospel is clear and consistent. Yet, why are there many who still don't understand the gospel? Why do so few believers regularly share the gospel? How does this story challenge you to be more faithful in sharing the gospel with the lost?

PRAYER:

Let's pray today that we will be more faithful in sharing the gospel.

PRAYER REQUESTS:

BI-MONTHLY MISSION PROJECT NOTES:

WEEK 18

Weekly Bible Reading: . . . . .Stories from Deuteronomy
Weekly Bible Study: . . . . Deuteronomy 6:1-15

DEUTERONOMY 6:1-25   [CIRCLE ONE: S P A C E]

Personal Study Notes: _____

_____

_____

_____

DEUTERONOMY 28:1-14   [CIRCLE ONE: S P A C E]

Personal Study Notes: _____

_____

_____

_____

DEUTERONOMY 28:15-68   [CIRCLE ONE: S P A C E]

Personal Study Notes: _____

_____

_____

_____

DEUTERONOMY 31:1-29   [CIRCLE ONE: S P A C E]

Personal Study Notes: _____

_____

_____

_____

DEUTERONOMY 34:1-12   [CIRCLE ONE: S P A C E]

Personal Study Notes: _____

_____

_____

_____

Read carefully one chapter of the Bible five days a week. In each chapter look for a . . .
Sin to Confess / **P**romise to Claim / **A**ttitude to Change / **C**ommand to Obey / **E**xample to Follow.

THE GREAT COMMANDMENT
(DEUTERONOMY 6:1-15)

WEEKLY ASSIGNMENTS:

Lead Prayer Time: _____

Tell the Story (Paraphrase): _____

Read the Text: _____

Facilitate Bible Study: _____

DISCUSSION QUESTIONS:

- Why is it important for people to have laws? What would the world be like if there were no laws?

- In our story, God gave His people clear commandments, statutes, and judgments. Why is this a reflection of God's love for us? What specific *promises to claim* does God give to those who keep them (v. 2-3)?

- The Great Commandment is known as the *Shema*, meaning to hear (v. 4-5). What does it mean to love the Lord your God with all your heart, with all your soul, and with all your strength? Read Matt. 22:34-38. What did Jesus say about this commandment? Why is this the greatest commandment?

- What were the Hebrews specifically instructed to do with these words (v. 6-9)? What does this imply about the importance of the biblical family? Why do you think Satan has always targeted families for his most aggressive attacks? What can you do to fortify your family against Satan's attacks?

- God instructed parents to "diligently" teach their children His words (v. 7-9). At what different times are parents instructed to teach their children? In what unique ways are parents instructed to teach them? How can we apply these instructions in our families today? How is your family doing in this?

- What things did God say He would give to the Hebrew families when He brings them into the land of promise (v. 10-12)? What things did He warn them not to do when they came into the land (v. 13-15)? What does it mean that God is a "jealous God?"

- In your life, what worldly gods challenge your affection for the one true God? What specific actions can you take to guard your heart from idolatry?

PRAYER:

Let's pray for one another today to love the Lord our God with all our heart, soul, and strength.

PRAYER REQUESTS:

BI-MONTHLY MISSION PROJECT NOTES:

WEEK 19

Weekly Bible Reading: .... Stories from Joshua
Weekly Bible Study: .... Joshua 2:1-21

JOSHUA 1:1-18   [CIRCLE ONE: S P A C E]
Personal Study Notes: _____

_____

_____

_____

JOSHUA 2:1-24   [CIRCLE ONE: S P A C E]
Personal Study Notes: _____

_____

_____

_____

JOSHUA 3:1-17   [CIRCLE ONE: S P A C E]
Personal Study Notes: _____

_____

_____

_____

JOSHUA 4:1-24   [CIRCLE ONE: S P A C E]
Personal Study Notes: _____

_____

_____

_____

JOSHUA 5:1-15   [CIRCLE ONE: S P A C E]
Personal Study Notes: _____

_____

_____

_____

Read carefully one chapter of the Bible five days a week. In each chapter look for a . . .
Sin to Confess / **P**romise to Claim / **A**ttitude to Change / **C**ommand to Obey / **E**xample to Follow.

THE FAITH OF RAHAB THE HARLOT
(JOSHUA 2:1-21)

WEEKLY ASSIGNMENTS:

Lead Prayer Time: _____

Tell the Story (Paraphrase): _____

Read the Text: _____

Facilitate Bible Study: _____

DISCUSSION QUESTIONS:

- Is anyone so far from God that he or she cannot be saved? Why or why not?

- In our story, Joshua and the children of Israel have a second chance to enter the Promised Land. How many spies did Joshua send to spy out the land and Jericho (v. 1a)? Why do you think he sent in only two spies this time?

- Where did the spies find lodging in Jericho (v. 1b)? Do you think they found this place of lodging by chance? Why or why not? Have you ever had a random encounter with someone that turned out to be a divine appointment? If so, what did you learn from this?

- What was Rahab's profession? What was her nationality? What did she do for the two Hebrew spies (v. 2-7)? Why do you think she did this?

- What did Rahab reveal to the spies about the inhabitants of Jericho (v. 8-9)? What had the people of Jericho heard about the God of Israel (v. 10)? What bold statement did Rahab make about the God of Israel (v. 11)? Do you think Rahab made a genuine profession of faith in God? Why or why not?

- What did Rahab request of the Hebrew spies (v. 12-13)? What was their response and what specific instructions did they give her (v. 14-18)? In what ways was the "scarlet cord" in the window reminiscent of the Passover? In what ways was it a foreshadowing of Christ?

- Read Heb. 11:31 and Matt. 1:5-6. What do these verses reveal about Rahab? How was her life changed? What does this teach us about the amazing grace of God? What lesson can we learn about our own attitude toward sinners?

- Do you know anyone who is so far away from God that salvation seems unlikely? How will you pray differently for him or her after today?

PRAYER:

Let's pray today for the salvation of someone you know who is far from God.

PRAYER REQUESTS:

BI-MONTHLY MISSION PROJECT NOTES:

WEEK 20

Weekly Bible Reading: .... Stories from Joshua
Weekly Bible Study: .... Joshua 6:1-27

JOSHUA 6:1-27 [CIRCLE ONE: S P A C E]
Personal Study Notes: _____
_____
_____
_____

JOSHUA 7:1-26 [CIRCLE ONE: S P A C E]
Personal Study Notes: _____
_____
_____
_____

JOSHUA 8:1-35 [CIRCLE ONE: S P A C E]
Personal Study Notes: _____
_____
_____
_____

JOSHUA 9:1-27 [CIRCLE ONE: S P A C E]
Personal Study Notes: _____
_____
_____
_____

JOSHUA 10:1-43 [CIRCLE ONE: S P A C E]
Personal Study Notes: _____
_____
_____
_____

Read carefully one chapter of the Bible five days a week. In each chapter look for a . . .
Sin to Confess / **P**romise to Claim / **A**ttitude to Change / **C**ommand to Obey / **E**xample to Follow.

THE FALL OF JERICHO
(JOSHUA 6:1-27)

WEEKLY ASSIGNMENTS:

Lead Prayer Time: _____

Tell the Story (Paraphrase): _____

Read the Text: _____

Facilitate Bible Study: _____

DISCUSSION QUESTIONS:

- What is the biggest challenge you have faced in life? How did you handle it?

- In our story, Joshua and the Israelites had to conquer the fortified city of Jericho in order to possess the Promised Land. Why do you think God put Jericho and its high walls in their path to the Promised Land?

- Why is it common for God to test the faith of His people? What tests of faith did the Israelites face in their first opportunity to possess the Promised Land? What is different about their response this second time?

- In spite of overwhelming odds against the Israelites, what promise did God give Joshua concerning Jericho (v. 1-2)? What specific instructions did God give Joshua to conquer Jericho (v. 3-5)? Why would this require great faith?

- God could have destroyed Jericho Himself, but why do you think He chose to involve the Israelites in the battle? What lessons would they learn from this?

- As *an example to follow*, what characteristics of godly leadership can we learn from Joshua (v. 6-21)? Rahab of Jericho was also a godly leader. What traits of godly leadership we can learn from Rahab (v. 22-25)? When godly men and women lead and people follow, what can be the result?

- Read Heb. 11:30-31. What common denominator is found in all godly leaders? Can you be a strong spiritual leader without faith? Why or why not?

- When we are following God's will, why do you think He sometimes allows a big obstacle to be in our path? What lessons can we learn from this story about how to handle life's obstacles?

- Are you facing any obstacle in your life today? How can we pray for you as you face this obstacle in faith?

PRAYER:

Let's pray for one another today to realize that no obstacle is too big for God.

PRAYER REQUESTS:

BI-MONTHLY MISSION PROJECT NOTES:

WEEK 21

Weekly Bible Reading: .... Stories from Joshua
Weekly Bible Study: .... Joshua 24:14-28

JOSHUA 14:1-15   [CIRCLE ONE: S P A C E]
Personal Study Notes: _____
_____
_____
_____

JOSHUA 20:1-9   [CIRCLE ONE: S P A C E]
Personal Study Notes: _____
_____
_____
_____

JOSHUA 22:1-34   [CIRCLE ONE: S P A C E]
Personal Study Notes: _____
_____
_____
_____

JOSHUA 23:16   [CIRCLE ONE: S P A C E]
Personal Study Notes: _____
_____
_____
_____

JOSHUA 24:1-33   [CIRCLE ONE: S P A C E]
Personal Study Notes: _____
_____
_____
_____

Read carefully one chapter of the Bible five days a week. In each chapter look for a . . .
Sin to Confess / **P**romise to Claim / **A**ttitude to Change / **C**ommand to Obey / **E**xample to Follow.

CHOOSE WHOM YOU WILL SERVE
(JOSHUA 24:14-28)

WEEKLY ASSIGNMENTS:

Lead Prayer Time: _____

Tell the Story (Paraphrase): _____

Read the Text: _____

Facilitate Bible Study: _____

DISCUSSION QUESTIONS:

- Why do some people feel a need to be popular? How important is this to you?

- In our story, Joshua gave his final challenge to the Israelites? How many times did he use the words "serve" or "served" in verses 14-15? Why do you think he put such a great emphasis on serving the Lord? Do you consider yourself a servant of the Lord? Why or why not?

- What major choice did Joshua place before the Israelites (v. 15a)? Why should this have been an easy choice for them to make? Regardless of what others did, what did Joshua boldly say about his choice (v. 15b)?

- In what ways did Joshua's words suggest a firm decision? In a world full of idolatry, why is it vital for our decision to serve the Lord to be a settled issue? In what ways does this choice mean that we might have to go against the crowd and make unpopular decisions?

- Who else did Joshua say was included in his choice to serve the Lord (v. 15b)? How is Joshua's leadership of his family an example to follow? In what ways might a family that serves the Lord have to go against popular culture?

- How did the Israelites respond to Joshua's challenge (v. 16-18)? At first, why do you think he expressed doubt about their sincerity (v. 19-20)? What was the Israelites final response to Joshua's challenge (v. 21-24)?

- What was the purpose of the large stone that Joshua set up at Shechem (v. 25-28)? When we make important commitments to God, why is it a good idea to have certain spiritual markers that help us remember them?

- Can you share about a recent stand you have taken for God that was not popular? If not, what might this say about your commitment to God?

PRAYER:

Let's pray today that each of us will have the courage to serve the Lord even when it's unpopular and that we will lead our families to do likewise.

PRAYER REQUESTS:

BI-MONTHLY MISSION PROJECT NOTES:

WEEK 22

Weekly Bible Reading: .... Stories from Judges
Weekly Bible Study: .... Judges 7:1-23

JUDGES 2:1-23
[CIRCLE ONE: S P A C E]

Personal Study Notes: _____

_____

_____

_____

JUDGES 3:1-31
[CIRCLE ONE: S P A C E]

Personal Study Notes: _____

_____

_____

_____

JUDGES 4:1-24
[CIRCLE ONE: S P A C E]

Personal Study Notes: _____

_____

_____

_____

JUDGES 6:1-40
[CIRCLE ONE: S P A C E]

Personal Study Notes: _____

_____

_____

_____

JUDGES 7:1-25
[CIRCLE ONE: S P A C E]

Personal Study Notes: _____

_____

_____

_____

Read carefully one chapter of the Bible five days a week. In each chapter look for a . . .
Sin to Confess / **P**romise to Claim / **A**ttitude to Change / **C**ommand to Obey / **E**xample to Follow.

GIDEON AND HIS ARMY
(JUDGES 7:1-23)

WEEKLY ASSIGNMENTS:

Lead Prayer Time: _____

Tell the Story (Paraphrase): _____

Read the Text: _____

Facilitate Bible Study: _____

DISCUSSION QUESTIONS:

- Can we ever be too big in our own eyes for God to use us? Why or why not? Can God ever be too small in our eyes for Him to use us? Why or why not?

- In our story, God used Gideon to assemble an army to deliver Israel from the tyranny of the Midianites. How big was Gideon's original army and what did God say about it (v. 1-2a)? Why did God say the army was too big (v. 2b)?

- Read Judges 6:14-16. When God called Gideon to this great task, why did Gideon think he was too small? What did God promise Gideon?

- In what two ways did God carve Gideon's army down to the right size (v. 3-6)? With how many men did God say He would defeat the Midianites (v. 7)?

- When Gideon went down to the camp of the Midianites, how large was the army of his enemy (v. 9-12)? How do you think he felt when he saw this? What encouraging words did Gideon hear at the camp of Midian and how did he respond (v. 13-15)? Why do you think God caused this to happen?

- In what miraculous way did God give Gideon's army a resounding victory (v. 16-23)? Read Judges 8:4. How many men did Gideon lose in the battle?

- As an attitude to change, what lessons can we learn from Gideon about the "bigness" of our God? What can we learn about thinking we are too weak or too small for the obstacles the enemy places before us?

- Read 1 Cor. 1:26-29. According to these verses, what kinds of people does God call to do His great works? In what three ways does God work to show that no human can boast in His presence?

- Is God leading you to do something or to face something bigger than you are? If so, what is it and how will you respond?

PRAYER:

Let's pray today for the faith to believe that we serve a big God.

PRAYER REQUESTS:

BI-MONTHLY MISSION PROJECT NOTES:

WEEK 23

Weekly Bible Reading: .... Stories from Judges
Weekly Bible Study: .... Judges 8:22-35

JUDGES 8:1-35
[CIRCLE ONE: S P A C E]

Personal Study Notes: _____

_____

_____

_____

JUDGES 9:1-57
[CIRCLE ONE: S P A C E]

Personal Study Notes: _____

_____

_____

_____

JUDGES 10:1-18
[CIRCLE ONE: S P A C E]

Personal Study Notes: _____

_____

_____

_____

JUDGES 11:1-40
[CIRCLE ONE: S P A C E]

Personal Study Notes: _____

_____

_____

_____

JUDGES 12:1-15
[CIRCLE ONE: S P A C E]

Personal Study Notes: _____

_____

_____

_____

Read carefully one chapter of the Bible five days a week. In each chapter look for a . . .
Sin to Confess / **P**romise to Claim / **A**ttitude to Change / **C**ommand to Obey / **E**xample to Follow.

GIDEON MAKES AN GOLDEN EPHOD
(JUDGES 8:22-35)

WEEKLY ASSIGNMENTS:

Lead Prayer Time: _____

Tell the Story (Paraphrase): _____

Read the Text: _____

Facilitate Bible Study: _____

DISCUSSION QUESTIONS:

- When you experience a great spiritual victory, why can it be a dangerous time in your life? What temptations might follow a spiritual victory?

- In our story, Gideon followed up a great spiritual victory by yielding to a prideful temptation. What did the people of Israel request of Gideon and why do you think he refused their request (v. 22-23)?

- Before Israel's victory, Gideon carefully listened and followed the Lord's instructions. Why do you think he began to act alone and stopped seeking the Lord's counsel? Why are the temptations of pride and self-righteousness particularly alluring after a spiritual victory?

- Acting on his own accord, what did Gideon request of the people (v. 24)? How did the people respond and how much did they give (v. 25-26)?

- Read. Ex. 29:4-5. What is an ephod (v. 27)? What do you think led Gideon to take the people's gifts and to make a golden ephod? What did the people do with this ephod? Why did this become "a snare" to Gideon and his family?

- Like many great leaders in Israel's past, why do you think Gideon failed to build an altar to God for His great deliverance over the Midianites? Why do you think he failed to call upon the people to be faithful to God?

- After Gideon died, what happened to the spiritual condition of the people of Israel (v. 33-34)? What happened in their attitude toward Gideon (v. 35)?

- Why was Gideon's legacy as a leader short lived? As *an attitude to change*, what happens when a leader becomes "big" in one's own eyes? How can we guard against these things? In what area of your life are you seeking a spiritual victory? How will you respond when God gives you victory?

PRAYER:

Let's pray today for wisdom to handle spiritual victories with humility and grace.

PRAYER REQUESTS:

BI-MONTHLY MISSION PROJECT NOTES:

WEEK 24

Weekly Bible Reading: .... Stories from Judges
Weekly Bible Study: .... Judges 16:1-22

JUDGES 13:1-25   [CIRCLE ONE: S P A C E]
Personal Study Notes: _____
_____
_____
_____

JUDGES 14:1-20   [CIRCLE ONE: S P A C E]
Personal Study Notes: _____
_____
_____
_____

JUDGES 15:1-20   [CIRCLE ONE: S P A C E]
Personal Study Notes: _____
_____
_____
_____

JUDGES 16:1-22   [CIRCLE ONE: S P A C E]
Personal Study Notes: _____
_____
_____
_____

JUDGES 16:23-31   [CIRCLE ONE: S P A C E]
Personal Study Notes: _____
_____
_____
_____

Read carefully one chapter of the Bible five days a week. In each chapter look for a . . .
Sin to Confess / **P**romise to Claim / **A**ttitude to Change / **C**ommand to Obey / **E**xample to Follow.

SAMSON AND DELILAH
(JUDGES 16:1-22)

WEEKLY ASSIGNMENTS:

Lead Prayer Time: _____

Tell the Story (Paraphrase): _____

Read the Text: _____

Facilitate Bible Study: _____

DISCUSSION QUESTIONS:

- Why do you think the world around us is growing more tolerant of sexual sin? What is sexual sin and has God's view toward it changed?

- In our story, Samson was a judge over Israel who was physically strong but spiritually weak. What sexual sin did Samson fall into while in Gaza (v. 1)?

- How can people of faith guard themselves from sexual temptation? What warning signs might indicate that someone is trying to seduce you sexually? How should you wisely respond to improper sexual seduction?

- What was Delilah's motive for attempting to seduce Samson (v. 4-5)? Why you think Samson fell so easily for her seductive ways (v. 6-20)?

- What obvious warning signs were there to indicate that Delilah's motives were not pure? Why do you think Samson continued to make the same mistakes and to fall for Delilah's traps?

- What physical and spiritual consequences did Samson experience because he fell for Delilah's seduction (v. 21-22)? Samson's moral failure greatly hurt himself, but how did it also adversely affect others around him?

- As *a sin to confess*, how might Samson's life had been different had he repented and turned away from this temptation? How might the lives of others be different? Whether it's lust over another person or looking at pornography, what consequences might we face if we give in to these traps?

- Why is a commitment to sexual purity a vital part of being a man or woman of God? What practical steps can we take to maintain sexual purity? How can we help one another in this area?

PRAYER:

Let's pray today for one another to wise up to sexual temptation and to stand strong in sexual purity.

PRAYER REQUESTS:

BI-MONTHLY MISSION PROJECT NOTES:

WEEK 25

Weekly Bible Reading: .... Stories from Ruth
Weekly Bible Study: .... Ruth 1:1-22

RUTH 1:1-22
[CIRCLE ONE: S P A C E]

Personal Study Notes: _____

_____

_____

_____

RUTH 2:1-13
[CIRCLE ONE: S P A C E]

Personal Study Notes: _____

_____

_____

_____

RUTH 2:13-23
[CIRCLE ONE: S P A C E]

Personal Study Notes: _____

_____

_____

_____

RUTH 3:1-18
[CIRCLE ONE: S P A C E]

Personal Study Notes: _____

_____

_____

_____

RUTH 4:1-22
[CIRCLE ONE: S P A C E]

Personal Study Notes: _____

_____

_____

_____

Read carefully one chapter of the Bible five days a week. In each chapter look for a . . .
Sin to Confess / **P**romise to Claim / **A**ttitude to Change / **C**ommand to Obey / **E**xample to Follow.

THE LOVE OF RUTH
(RUTH 1:1-22)

WEEKLY ASSIGNMENTS:

Lead Prayer Time: _____

Tell the Story (Paraphrase): _____

Read the Text: _____

Facilitate Bible Study: _____

DISCUSSION QUESTIONS:

- What is your favorite love song? Why do we like love songs and stories?

- In our story, Ruth and her mother-in-law, Naomi, experienced great tragedy in land of Moab, but love carried them through it. What town in Judah was Naomi from and what caused and her family to go to the land of the Moab (v. 1-2)? What calamities did she experience there (v. 3-5)?

- What different emotions do you think Naomi experienced? When have you lost someone close to you? What things helped you deal with your great loss? How does our faith help us get through times of grief?

- What did Naomi encourage her daughter-in-laws to do (v. 6-9)? How did Orpah and Ruth respond (v. 10-14)? What beautiful vow of commitment did Ruth make to Naomi (v. 15-18)? What specific promises did Ruth make? Do you think Ruth made a genuine profession of faith in God? Why or why not?

- As *an example to follow*, in what ways do you think Naomi's faith influenced Ruth? Why is our witness for God more powerful during times of trial than any other time?

- Naomi left Judah during a time of famine and returned "at the beginning of barley harvest" (v. 19-22)? Read Ruth 2:1-3 and Matt. 1:5-6. What significance does the season of "barley harvest" have in relation to God's providence over Naomi and Ruth? What two great kings are from the bloodline of Ruth?

- What can we learn from this about the providence of God in our times of trial? In what ways have you reached out to help others who have experienced the loss of a family member? How could our D-Group minister to someone in this situation?

PRAYER:

Let's pray today for perseverance and faith for someone we know who is going through a time of trial.

PRAYER REQUESTS:

BI-MONTHLY MISSION PROJECT NOTES:

WEEK 26

Weekly Bible Reading: .... Stories from 1 Samuel
Weekly Bible Study: .... 1 Samuel 1:3-20

1 SAMUEL 1:1-28   [CIRCLE ONE: S P A C E]
Personal Study Notes: _____
_____
_____
_____

1 SAMUEL 2:1-36   [CIRCLE ONE: S P A C E]
Personal Study Notes: _____
_____
_____
_____

1 SAMUEL 3:1-21   [CIRCLE ONE: S P A C E]
Personal Study Notes: _____
_____
_____
_____

1 SAMUEL 4:1-22   [CIRCLE ONE: S P A C E]
Personal Study Notes: _____
_____
_____
_____

1 SAMUEL 5:1-12   [CIRCLE ONE: S P A C E]
Personal Study Notes: _____
_____
_____
_____

Read carefully one chapter of the Bible five days a week. In each chapter look for a . . .
Sin to Confess / **P**romise to Claim / **A**ttitude to Change / **C**ommand to Obey / **E**xample to Follow.

HANNAH PRAYS FOR A SON
(1 SAMUEL 1:3-20)

WEEKLY ASSIGNMENTS:

Lead Prayer Time: _____

Tell the Story (Paraphrase): _____

Read the Text: _____

Facilitate Bible Study: _____

DISCUSSION QUESTIONS:

- What do you think is the difference between a prayer request and a prayer burden? In what ways do we pray differently over a prayer burden?

- In our story, a man named Elkanah had two wives, Hannah and Peninnah. Is it God's will for a man to have more than one wife? Why or why not? In this polygamist relationship, what problems arose between Hannah and Peninnah (v. 3-8)? What caused Hannah to weep and go without eating?

- What vow did Hannah make to the Lord as she wept and prayed (v. 9-11)? How was Eli the Priest mistaken about Hannah (v. 12-14)? How did she respond to Eli's misjudgment (v. 15-16)?

- What word of assurance did Eli give Hannah (v. 17)? How is Hannah's response a reflection of her faith (v. 18-19a)? How did God answer her prayer (v. 19b-20)? What does it mean to "pour out your soul before the Lord" (v. 15b)? Do you ever pour out your soul to the Lord? Why or why not?

- Read Luke 18:1-8. How is Hannah like the "persistent widow" in Jesus' parable? As and *example to follow*, what important lessons on prayer can we learn from Hannah and the persistent widow?

- Why do you think some miracles only come in response to persistent prayer? What relationship does persistent prayer have to our faith? Can you share about a time when you have persistently poured out your soul to the Lord over a prayer burden? How has God answered this prayer?

- Every week our D-Group prays for revival and spiritual awakening in our land. Why is it important for this to be a persistent prayer burden for all believers?

PRAYER:

Let's pray today that God will give us a persistent prayer burden for revival and spiritual awakening in our land.

PRAYER REQUESTS:

BI-MONTHLY MISSION PROJECT NOTES:

WEEK 27

Weekly Bible Reading: .... Stories from 1 Samuel
Weekly Bible Study: .... 1 Samuel 8:1-22

1 SAMUEL 6:1-21 [CIRCLE ONE: S P A C E]

Personal Study Notes: _____

_____

_____

_____

1 SAMUEL 7:1-17 [CIRCLE ONE: S P A C E]

Personal Study Notes: _____

_____

_____

_____

1 SAMUEL 8:1-22 [CIRCLE ONE: S P A C E]

Personal Study Notes: _____

_____

_____

_____

1 SAMUEL 9:1-27 [CIRCLE ONE: S P A C E]

Personal Study Notes: _____

_____

_____

_____

1 SAMUEL 10:1-27 [CIRCLE ONE: S P A C E]

Personal Study Notes: _____

_____

_____

_____

Read carefully one chapter of the Bible five days a week. In each chapter look for a . . .
Sin to Confess / **P**romise to Claim / **A**ttitude to Change / **C**ommand to Obey / **E**xample to Follow.

ISRAEL DEMANDS A KING
(1 SAMUEL 8:1-22)

WEEKLY ASSIGNMENTS:

Lead Prayer Time: _____

Tell the Story (Paraphrase): _____

Read the Text: _____

Facilitate Bible Study: _____

DISCUSSION QUESTIONS:

- Why are positions of power potentially hazardous to our faith? What temptations come with positions of power?

- In our story, the Israelites demanded for a king. Samuel had made his sons, Joel and Abijah, Judges over the land, but why was this an unwise decision (v. 1-3)? How did this fuel Israel's misguided desire for a king (v. 4-5)?

- Why did Israel's request for a king displease Samuel and God (v. 6-8)? Why do you think God told Samuel to give them what they asked for (v. 9)? What specific warnings did Samuel give the people about the ways of a king (v. 10-18)? Do we want God to always give us what we ask for? Why or why not?

- Why did the people refuse to obey the voice of Samuel (v. 19-20)? *As an attitude to change*, why is a desire to be like others a dangerous trap for any believer? Why must believers embrace the call to be separate from the world? When we are separate from the world, how does this glorify God?

- When the people said they wanted a king who would "go out before us and fight our battles," why must this have been very offensive to God (v. 20b)? In today's world, why is it important for us not to put our trust in any earthly leader?

- It is often said, "Be careful what you ask for." How are these words relevant in this situation? When godly people warn you about the decisions you are making, how should you respond? Why is it foolish to ignore this warning?

- When God responds with a "no" to our prayer requests, why should we respond with faith and gratitude? Can you share about a time when God said, "No," and you realized it was for the best?

PRAYER:

Let's thank God today for all the times when He has blessed us by responding to our prayer requests by answering with, "No."

PRAYER REQUESTS:

BI-MONTHLY MISSION PROJECT NOTES:

WEEK 28

Weekly Bible Reading: . . . . Stories from 1 Samuel
Weekly Bible Study: . . . . 1 Samuel 13:5-14

1 SAMUEL 11:1-15
[CIRCLE ONE: S P A C E]

Personal Study Notes: _____

_____

_____

_____

1 SAMUEL 12:1-25
[CIRCLE ONE: S P A C E]

Personal Study Notes: _____

_____

_____

_____

1 SAMUEL 13:1-23
[CIRCLE ONE: S P A C E]

Personal Study Notes: _____

_____

_____

_____

1 SAMUEL 14:1-52
[CIRCLE ONE: S P A C E]

Personal Study Notes: _____

_____

_____

_____

1 SAMUEL 15:1-35
[CIRCLE ONE: S P A C E]

Personal Study Notes: _____

_____

_____

_____

Read carefully one chapter of the Bible five days a week. In each chapter look for a . . .
Sin to Confess / **P**romise to Claim / **A**ttitude to Change / **C**ommand to Obey / **E**xample to Follow.

SAUL'S IMPATIENCE AND DISOBEDIENCE
(1 SAMUEL 13:5-14)

WEEKLY ASSIGNMENTS:

Lead Prayer Time: _____

Tell the Story (Paraphrase): _____

Read the Text: _____

Facilitate Bible Study: _____

DISCUSSION QUESTIONS:

• When people make mistakes, why do they often give excuses? What is the dumbest excuse you have ever heard? Why is it better to take ownership of our mistakes than to make excuses?

• In our story, King Saul grew impatient and disobeyed the Lord. What circumstances caused Saul to grow impatient (v. 5-8)? Does his impatience seem reasonable? Why or why not? Why is it often hard to wait on the Lord?

• Read 1 Sam. 10:8. In this verse, what specific instructions did Saul receive from Samuel? How many days was Saul instructed to wait for Samuel? What part of Samuel's instructions did Saul disobey (v. 8-9)?

• What excuses did Saul give for his actions (v. 10-12)? How did Samuel reply to his excuses (v. 13)? What were the consequences of his actions (v. 14)? In God's eyes, why is partial obedience the same as disobedience? In what ways can partial obedience be more dangerous than disobedience?

- Read 1 Sam. 15:7-9, 17-23. In what ways did Saul continued to struggle with issues of obedience. *As an attitude to change*, what important life lessons did Saul learn about partial obedience? How can we apply this in our lives today?

- When Samuel said that "the Lord has sought out a man after His own heart" to replace Saul as king, to whom was he referring (v. 14)? David had his own issues, but what does it mean to be a person after God's own heart?

- Do you consider yourself a person after God's own heart? Why or why not? In what ways is obedience to God a matter of the heart?

- In our relationship with God, why is it better to obey than to sacrifice? Why is it better to wait on God than to rush ahead with our own plans? In what ways can you continue to grow into a person after God's own heart?

PRAYER:

Let's pray for one another today to be a person after God's own heart.

PRAYER REQUESTS:

BI-MONTHLY MISSION PROJECT NOTES:

WEEK 29

Weekly Bible Reading: .... Stories from 1 Samuel
Weekly Bible Study: .... 1 Samuel 17:31-58

1 SAMUEL 16:1-23   [CIRCLE ONE: S P A C E]
Personal Study Notes: _____
_____
_____
_____

1 SAMUEL 17:1-58   [CIRCLE ONE: S P A C E]
Personal Study Notes: _____
_____
_____
_____

1 SAMUEL 18:1-30   [CIRCLE ONE: S P A C E]
Personal Study Notes: _____
_____
_____
_____

1 SAMUEL 19:1-24   [CIRCLE ONE: S P A C E]
Personal Study Notes: _____
_____
_____
_____

1 SAMUEL 20:1-42   [CIRCLE ONE: S P A C E]
Personal Study Notes: _____
_____
_____
_____

Read carefully one chapter of the Bible five days a week. In each chapter look for a . . .
Sin to Confess / **P**romise to Claim / **A**ttitude to Change / **C**ommand to Obey / **E**xample to Follow.

DAVID AND GOLIATH
(1 SAMUEL 17:31-58)

WEEKLY ASSIGNMENTS:

Lead Prayer Time: _____

Tell the Story (Paraphrase): _____

Read the Text: _____

Facilitate Bible Study: _____

DISCUSSION QUESTIONS:

- Why is it easy to dislike a bully? Why is it important to stand up to a bully?

- In our story, David was a young shepherd boy when he stood up to the giant Philistine, Goliath. When David volunteered to fight Goliath, for what reasons did King Saul say he was "not able" (v. 31-33)? Have others ever discouraged you from doing something God wanted you to do? Can you share about it?

- How did David answer Saul's discouragement (v. 34-37)? How had God prepared young David for this moment in his life? Can you share about a trial or challenge in your life that prepared you for something greater later on?

- Saul attempted to clothe David with his own armor, but why did this not work for David (v. 38-39)? What did David choose as his weapon (v. 40)? Why can we not fight our own battles with another person's armor?

- Read 1 Sam. 17:4-7. How is Goliath described? How is David described (v. 42)? How do you think Goliath felt about his chances against David?

- What words of intimidation did Goliath speak to David (v. 43-44)? What was David's response to Goliath (v. 45-47)? Whose battle did David say this was and how did this change David's chances for victory (v. 47b)?

- With one stone Goliath was killed, but why do you think David had chosen five stones from the brook (v. 48-50)? Since Goliath was already dead, why do you think David took the giant's sword and cut his head off (v. 51a)?

- What did the Philistines do when they saw their champion dead (v. 51b)? Why do you think David kept Goliath's armor (v. 54)?

- *As an example to follow*, what lessons can we learn from David about fighting our own giants? What particular giant you are facing today?

PRAYER:

Let's pray for one another today that we will have the courage to face our giants and to overcome them in faith.

PRAYER REQUESTS:

BI-MONTHLY MISSION PROJECT NOTES:

WEEK 30

1 SAMUEL 21:1-15
[CIRCLE ONE: S P A C E]

Personal Study Notes: _____

_____

_____

_____

1 SAMUEL 22:1-23
[CIRCLE ONE: S P A C E]

Personal Study Notes: _____

_____

_____

_____

1 SAMUEL 23:1-29
[CIRCLE ONE: S P A C E]

Personal Study Notes: _____

_____

_____

_____

1 SAMUEL 24:1-22
[CIRCLE ONE: S P A C E]

Personal Study Notes: _____

_____

_____

_____

1 SAMUEL 25:1-44
[CIRCLE ONE: S P A C E]

Personal Study Notes: _____

_____

_____

_____

Read carefully one chapter of the Bible five days a week. In each chapter look for a . . .
Sin to Confess / **P**romise to Claim / **A**ttitude to Change / **C**ommand to Obey / **E**xample to Follow.

DAVID SPARES SAUL'S LIFE
(1 SAMUEL 24:1-22)

WEEKLY ASSIGNMENTS:

Lead Prayer Time: _____

Tell the Story (Paraphrase): _____

Read the Text: _____

Facilitate Bible Study: _____

DISCUSSION QUESTIONS:

- Have you ever had a real enemy? If so, how did it make you feel? What kinds of things cause people to become enemies?

- In our story, David spared the life of King Saul. What unique opportunity did David have to harm Saul (v. 1-3)? Instead of killing him, what did David do to Saul (v. 4)? What did David tell his men about his decision (v. 5-7)?

- What did David mean by describing Saul as "the Lord's anointed?" What role did godly respect and faith play in David's decision to spare Saul? Even when "the Lord's anointed" is in the wrong, why must we still show respect?

- Read 1 Sam. 18:28-29. Why did King Saul view David as an enemy? Do you think David deserved this treatment? How do you think David must have felt?

- What evidence did David present to Saul as proof of his grace and kindness toward him (v. 8-12)? What do you think is the meaning of the ancient proverb that David quoted to King Saul (v. 13)?

- Read Matthew 5:43-44. How do these words of Jesus compare to the ancient proverb that David quoted? Why is it hard to love our enemies and to be kind to them? Even though it is hard, why is it important for us to do this?

- How did Saul respond to David's kindness (v. 16-19)? Realizing that David would become the next King, what request did Saul make of David (v. 20-21)? How is David's response to this request another example of his kindness and respect (v. 22)?

- *As an example to follow*, what can we learn from David about dealing with our enemies? How can we pray for you today in your personal dealings with an enemy?

PRAYER:

Let's pray for one another today to have the faith and courage to love our enemies.

PRAYER REQUESTS:

BI-MONTHLY MISSION PROJECT NOTES:

WEEK 31

Weekly Bible Reading: .... Stories from 1 Samuel
Weekly Bible Study: .... 1 Samuel 28:3-19

1 SAMUEL 26:1-15   [CIRCLE ONE: S P A C E]
Personal Study Notes: _____
_____
_____
_____

1 SAMUEL 27:1-12   [CIRCLE ONE: S P A C E]
Personal Study Notes: _____
_____
_____
_____

1 SAMUEL 28:1-25   [CIRCLE ONE: S P A C E]
Personal Study Notes: _____
_____
_____
_____

1 SAMUEL 29:1-11   [CIRCLE ONE: S P A C E]
Personal Study Notes: _____
_____
_____
_____

1 SAMUEL 30:1-30   [CIRCLE ONE: S P A C E]
Personal Study Notes: _____
_____
_____
_____

Read carefully one chapter of the Bible five days a week. In each chapter look for a . . .
Sin to Confess / **P**romise to Claim / **A**ttitude to Change / **C**ommand to Obey / **E**xample to Follow.

SAUL CONSULTS A MEDIUM

(1 SAMUEL 28:3-19)

WEEKLY ASSIGNMENTS:

Lead Prayer Time: _____

Tell the Story (Paraphrase): _____

Read the Text: _____

Facilitate Bible Study: _____

DISCUSSION QUESTIONS:

- Have you ever experimented with the occult? If so, what happened in these experiences and how did you feel about them? Why do you think there is much fascination with the occult today?

- In our story, King Saul consulted a medium at En-dor. What circumstances provoked King Saul to consult the medium at En-dor (v. 3-7)? Do you think Saul knew his actions were wrong? Why or why not?

- Read Lev. 19:31; 20:6, 27, Deut. 18:9-12. What is a medium and what does God clearly say about consulting mediums? Why do you think God forbids such practices? Why is the occult dangerous?

- Why do you think Saul disguised himself when went to the medium (v. 8)? What decision had Saul previously made about mediums and spiritists in Israel (v. 9)? What do you think causes someone to return to a past sin?

- How did the medium respond when she first saw the spirit of Samuel (v. 10-14)? Why do you think she was so surprised and fearful? What was Samuel's appearance? Do you think this was really Samuel? Why or why not?

- We know that demonic spirits are real, but it is extremely rare for the spirit of a departed saint to return to earth. Can you think of any other instances in the Bible when this happened? If so, when?

- Why do you think God would permit the spirit of Samuel to return to Saul in this instance? What bad news did Samuel have for Saul (v. 15-19)?

- From this story and other teachings in the Bible, why should we never experiment with the occult or seek out departed spirits? On the positive side, what good news is reinforced by this story about the death of God's people?

PRAYER:

Let's pray and give God praise for the reality of life after death and for believers who have died and are already with the Lord.

PRAYER REQUESTS:

BI-MONTHLY MISSION PROJECT NOTES:

Weekly Bible Reading: .... Stories from 1 & 2 Samuel
Weekly Bible Study: .... 2 Samuel 2:1-11

1 SAMUEL 31:1-13   [CIRCLE ONE: S P A C E]

Personal Study Notes: _____

_____

_____

_____

2 SAMUEL 1:1-27   [CIRCLE ONE: S P A C E]

Personal Study Notes: _____

_____

_____

_____

2 SAMUEL 2:1-32   [CIRCLE ONE: S P A C E]

Personal Study Notes: _____

_____

_____

_____

2 SAMUEL 3:1-39   [CIRCLE ONE: S P A C E]

Personal Study Notes: _____

_____

_____

_____

2 SAMUEL 4:1-12   [CIRCLE ONE: S P A C E]

Personal Study Notes: _____

_____

_____

_____

Read carefully one chapter of the Bible five days a week. In each chapter look for a . . .
Sin to Confess / **P**romise to Claim / **A**ttitude to Change / **C**ommand to Obey / **E**xample to Follow.

DAVID HAS A RIVAL KING
(2 SAMUEL 2:1-11)

WEEKLY ASSIGNMENTS:

Lead Prayer Time: _____

Tell the Story (Paraphrase): _____

Read the Text: _____

Facilitate Bible Study: _____

DISCUSSION QUESTIONS:

- When you have an important decision to make, how much time to you spend seeking the counsel of the Lord? In what ways do you seek the counsel of the Lord? In what ways does He answer?

- In our story, David inquired of the Lord concerning his return to Judah after Saul's death. What two things did God reveal to David in response (v. 1-2)? How did David respond to God's leadership (v. 3)?

- Read 1 Sam. 13:14. How does David's example in this instance reveal that he is a man after God's own heart? *As a sin to confess*, what does it indicate when we make decisions apart from God's counsel?

- After David returned to Hebron, what honor did the men of Judah give him (v. 4a)? Because David sought after the

Lord instead of seeking the crown, what conclusions can we draw from this about his personal walk with God?

- Even though Saul was David's enemy, how did David respond to those who honored Saul in his death (v. 4b-5)? Why do you think he responded this way? In what ways does this quality in David's life make him someone easy to respect?

- Though it was God's will for David to be the King, what immediate conflict arose from a rival for the throne (v. 8-11)? Why is following God's will often difficult and filled with challenges?

- Can you share about a time in your own life when following God's will was difficult and challenging? In what ways did you grow spiritually through this personal experience?

- When God's will is challenging, why is it important for us to persevere? What roles does our faith play in our perseverance?

PRAYER:

Let's pray for one another today to have steadfast perseverance in following God's will even when it is difficult and challenging.

PRAYER REQUESTS:

BI-MONTHLY MISSION PROJECT NOTES:

WEEK 33

Weekly Bible Reading: .... Stories from 2 Samuel
Weekly Bible Study: .... 2 Samuel 9:1-13

2 SAMUEL 5:1-25 [CIRCLE ONE: S P A C E]
Personal Study Notes: _____
_____
_____
_____

2 SAMUEL 6:1-23 [CIRCLE ONE: S P A C E]
Personal Study Notes: _____
_____
_____
_____

2 SAMUEL 7:1-29 [CIRCLE ONE: S P A C E]
Personal Study Notes: _____
_____
_____
_____

2 SAMUEL 8:1-18 [CIRCLE ONE: S P A C E]
Personal Study Notes: _____
_____
_____
_____

2 SAMUEL 9:1-13 [CIRCLE ONE: S P A C E]
Personal Study Notes: _____
_____
_____
_____

Read carefully one chapter of the Bible five days a week. In each chapter look for a . . .
Sin to Confess / **P**romise to Claim / **A**ttitude to Change / **C**ommand to Obey / **E**xample to Follow.

DAVID'S KINDNESS TO MEPHIBOSHETH
(2 SAMUEL 9:1-13)

WEEKLY ASSIGNMENTS:

Lead Prayer Time: _____

Tell the Story (Paraphrase): _____

Read the Text: _____

Facilitate Bible Study: _____

John 1:12-13

DISCUSSION QUESTIONS:

• What is the most expensive and unexpected gift anyone has ever given to you? How did it make you feel when you received this gift?

• In our story, David shows the kindness of God to a descendent of Saul named Mephibosheth. What provoked David to show "kindness" to anyone left of the house of Saul (v. 1)? Read 1 Sam. 18:1-4. Who was Jonathan and why do you think David continued to think fondly of him?

• Who was the one person left of the house of Saul, and what was unique about him (v. 2-4)? Read 2 Sam. 4:4. What ill-fated incident had happened to him?

• At a time when kings would kill all rivals to their throne, what do you think Mephibosheth must have thought and felt when David sent for him? How did Mephibosheth respond when he first met King David (v. 5-6)?

- What good news did David share with Mephibosheth (v. 7)? Did he in any way earn or deserve David's extraordinary kindness (v. 8)? Why or Why not?

- In what ways did Mephibosheth become like one of David's own sons (v. 9-13)? From an obscure place like Lo-debar to feasting daily at the king's table, how do you think Mephibosheth's outlook on life must have changed?

- In what ways is the grace that David showed Mephibosheth similar to the grace that God offers all sinners? David showed grace and kindness for Jonathan's sake. In whose name does God offer His grace to us?

- When we receive God's grace through faith in Jesus Christ, in what ways do we become like one of God's own sons or daughters? Have you received God's great gift of grace through faith in Christ? If so, how does this present us with an *attitude to change*?

PRAYER:

Let's pray today that we will always remember Who we belong to and that we will live like sons and daughters of the King.

PRAYER REQUESTS:

BI-MONTHLY MISSION PROJECT NOTES:

WEEK (34)

Ps 119:18 Open my eyes, that I may behold wonderous things out of your law.

Weekly Bible Reading: .... Stories from 2 Samuel
Weekly Bible Study: .... 2 Samuel 11:1-17

2 SAMUEL 10:1-19   [CIRCLE ONE: S P A C E]
Personal Study Notes: _____
_____
_____
_____

2 SAMUEL 11:1-27   [CIRCLE ONE: S P A C E]
Personal Study Notes: _Ps 51 David's plea for forgiveness_
James 1:14-15 temptation is the pull of man's own evil
_____thoughts and wishes_____
Lev 20:22 Lev 20:10 penalty for adultery is death for both

2 SAMUEL 12:1-31   [CIRCLE ONE: S P A C E]
Personal Study Notes: _____
_____
_____
_____

2 SAMUEL 13:1-39   [CIRCLE ONE: S P A C E]
Personal Study Notes: _____
_____
_____
_____

2 SAMUEL 14:1-33   [CIRCLE ONE: S P A C E]
Personal Study Notes: _____
_____
_____
_____

Read carefully one chapter of the Bible five days a week. In each chapter look for a . . .
Sin to Confess / **P**romise to Claim / **A**ttitude to Change / **C**ommand to Obey / **E**xample to Follow.

DAVID AND BATHSHEBA
(2 SAMUEL 11:1-17)

WEEKLY ASSIGNMENTS:

Lead Prayer Time: _____

Tell the Story (Paraphrase): _____

Read the Text: _____

Facilitate Bible Study: _____

DISCUSSION QUESTIONS:

- Can you share about a time when you found yourself at the wrong place at the wrong time? How are times like this a test of our faith?

- In our story, King David found himself at the wrong place at the wrong time. At the time "when kings go out to battle," why do you think David remained at home (v. 1)? What "happened" one afternoon that caused David to be overcome by lust (v. 2)?

- Do you think Bathsheba was totally innocent in this situation? Why or why not? What role do you think Satan played in this situation? What should he have done when he saw this beautiful woman bathing? David conquered Goliath, why could he not conquer lust?

- What did David's unchecked lust cause him to do (v. 3-4)? When Bathsheba became pregnant, what greater evil did David do in attempt to cover up his sin (v. 5-17)? How many people were affected by David's sinful choices?

- Why is it important for us to quickly "bounce our eyes" and turn away from lustful situations? What happens when we linger over lustful situations?

- In a sex-crazed world, how can we guard ourselves against pornography? Why is porn so dangerous? How can we guard ourselves against sexual sins such as adultery or pre-marital sex? What's so bad about these sins?

- Read Psalm 51-13. In this Psalm of repentance, David gives us an *example to follow*. When we sin greatly, how can we experience forgiveness with God?

earn your mistakes

- How we help one another in our battle against lust? How can we pray for you regarding your fight against lust?

PRAYER:

Let's pray for one another today that we will bounce our eyes away from lust and flee from lustful situations.

PRAYER REQUESTS:

BI-MONTHLY MISSION PROJECT NOTES:

Weekly Bible Reading: .... Stories from 2 Samuel
Weekly Bible Study: .... 2 Samuel 19:1-8

2 SAMUEL 15:1-37   [CIRCLE ONE: S P A C E]
Personal Study Notes: _____

_____

_____

_____

2 SAMUEL 16:1-23   [CIRCLE ONE: S P A C E]

So David gave all of Mephibosheth's land to Ziba

Personal Study Notes: Ziba vs 1-4 lied - David gave ½ of Mephibosheth's land to Ziba 19:29

Shime-i vs 5-14 threw stones at David

David spared Shime-i's life

_____

2 SAMUEL 17:1-29   [CIRCLE ONE: S P A C E]
Personal Study Notes: _____

_____

_____

_____

2 SAMUEL 18:1-33   [CIRCLE ONE: S P A C E]
Personal Study Notes: _____

_____

_____

_____

2 SAMUEL 19:1-43   [CIRCLE ONE: S P A C E]
Personal Study Notes: _____

_____

_____

_____

Read carefully one chapter of the Bible five days a week. In each chapter look for a . . .
Sin to Confess / **P**romise to Claim / **A**ttitude to Change / **C**ommand to Obey / **E**xample to Follow.

DAVID MOURNS FOR ABSALOM
(2 SAMUEL 19:1-8)

WEEKLY ASSIGNMENTS:

Lead Prayer Time: _____

Tell the Story (Paraphrase): _____

Read the Text: _____

Facilitate Bible Study: _____

DISCUSSION QUESTIONS:

- What is the worst decision you have ever made? What regrets did you have over this decision and how did you handle these regrets?

- In our story, David mourns the loss of his son, Absalom, in spite of the great victory his army had experienced. In what ways was David continuing to suffer the painful consequences of his sinful decision with Bathsheba?

- Read 2 Samuel 14:28. How long did Absalom live in Jerusalem without coming into the presence of his father the King? When a father and son become estranged from one another, why does this often lead to rebellion? How might David's immense sorrow have been avoided (v. 1-3)?

- David's deep cry, "O my son Absalom, O Absalom, my son, my son," is likely a cry of loss and regret (v. 4). How can we avoid such painful regrets related to our own families? Perhaps David thought he had more time, but why is procrastinating to reconcile broken relationships an *attitude to change*?

• Who was Joab and what point of contention did he raise with David (v. 5-7)? Do you think he was being insensitive or did he have a valid point? Why or why not?

• When we are self-absorbed with our own hurts and pains, why is it important to have someone like Joab in our lives? Why must we sometimes play the role of Joab in someone else's life?

• How did David respond to Joab's counsel (v. 8)? When we are overcome with troubles, why must we continue to be considerate of others who love us?

• If you have a severed relationship with a friend or family member, what first step should you take toward reconciliation? When should you take this step?

PRAYER:

Let's pray for one another today to always be willing to take the first step toward reconciliation in a broken relationship.

PRAYER REQUESTS:

Hillary
Robin Kensey
Suzanne — Weston's M-N-L
Robin Lodge kidney
Ellen McCranie
Jennifer Neel (JR) pg

BI-MONTHLY MISSION PROJECT NOTES:

WEEK 36

2 SAMUEL 20:1-26
[CIRCLE ONE: S P A C E]
*Personal Study Notes:*_____
_____
_____
_____

2 SAMUEL 21:1-22
[CIRCLE ONE: S P A C E]
*Personal Study Notes:*_____
_____
_____
_____

2 SAMUEL 22:1-51
[CIRCLE ONE: S P A C E]
*Personal Study Notes:*_____
_____
_____
_____

2 SAMUEL 23:1-39
[CIRCLE ONE: S P A C E]
*Personal Study Notes:*_____
_____
_____
_____

2 SAMUEL 24:1-25
[CIRCLE ONE: S P A C E]
*Personal Study Notes:*_____
_____
_____
_____

Read carefully one chapter of the Bible five days a week. In each chapter look for a . . .
Sin to Confess / **P**romise to Claim / **A**ttitude to Change / **C**ommand to Obey / **E**xample to Follow.

DAVID'S MIGHTY MEN
(2 SAMUEL 23:8-17)

WEEKLY ASSIGNMENTS:

Lead Prayer Time: _____

Tell the Story (Paraphrase): _____

Read the Text: _____

Facilitate Bible Study: _____

DISCUSSION QUESTIONS:

- Who is your favorite super hero and why? Why do you think we like super heroes so much?

- In our story, we read about some real heroes who were known as David's "mighty men." What were these men's names and for what particular act of courage was each one remembered (8-12)?

- After these men accomplished heroic deeds, twice it says, "and the Lord brought about a great victory" (v. 10, 12). What does this imply about the amazing deeds of these men? Why is this important?

- When David was in the stronghold at the cave of Adullam and he thirsted for water, what did three of his mighty men do for him (v. 13-16a)? How did David respond to the bravery of these men who risked their lives for him (v. 16b-17)? Why do you think these men were so loyal to David?

- In the church today, who is our enemy and what can we learn from David's mighty men about our fight against this enemy? Why do you think men and women in the church today often lack spiritual strength and courage?

- We need spiritual warriors today of all ages and genders. How does one become a spiritual warrior and how does God use them in His work?

- Do you desire to be a spiritual warrior for Christ, and in what ways are you growing toward becoming one? As one loyal to Jesus, what are some things you feel He is leading you to do that will require faith and courage?

- How is this group helping you to grow as a spiritual warrior? In your fight against the enemy, what is one main thing we can pray for you about today?

PRAYER:

Let's pray for one another today to grow as spiritual warriors and to be strong in our fight against the enemy.

PRAYER REQUESTS:

BI-MONTHLY MISSION PROJECT NOTES:

WEEK (37)

next week 7, 8, 9, 10 & 11

1 KINGS 1:1-53   [CIRCLE ONE: S P A C E]
Personal Study Notes: _____
_____
_____
_____

1 KINGS 3:1-28   [CIRCLE ONE: S P A C E]
Personal Study Notes: _____
_____
_____
_____

1 KINGS 9:1-28   [CIRCLE ONE: S P A C E]
Personal Study Notes: _____
_____
_____
_____

1 KINGS 11:1-43   [CIRCLE ONE: S P A C E]
Personal Study Notes: _____
_____
_____
_____

1 KINGS 12:1-33   [CIRCLE ONE: S P A C E]
Personal Study Notes: _____
_____
_____
_____

Read carefully one chapter of the Bible five days a week. In each chapter look for a . . .
Sin to Confess / **P**romise to Claim / **A**ttitude to Change / **C**ommand to Obey / **E**xample to Follow.

SOLOMON PRAYS FOR WISDOM
(1 KINGS 3:5-14)

WEEKLY ASSIGNMENTS:

Lead Prayer Time: _____

Tell the Story (Paraphrase): _____

Read the Text: _____

Facilitate Bible Study: _____

DISCUSSION QUESTIONS:

- Who would you consider to be the wisest person you know and how has your life been influenced by this person's wisdom?

- In our story, David's son, Solomon, had become the King of Israel and the Lord appeared to him in a dream. What did the Lord ask of Solomon in this dream (v. 5)? What was Solomon's response (v. 6-9)?

- What do you think is the difference between wisdom and knowledge? What difference is there between "worldly wisdom" and "godly wisdom?" Why did Solomon say that he needed godly wisdom (v. 9)?

- In his wisdom King Solomon wrote the book of Proverbs. Read Proverbs 9:10. What did Solomon say was the beginning of wisdom? In what way did Solomon's request for wisdom reflect the principle of Proverbs 9:10.

- Why is asking God for wisdom better than asking Him for long life or riches? Since God was please with Solomon's request, what other blessings did He promise to give him (v. 10-13)? What conditions did God place on His promise to lengthen Solomon's days (v. 14)? Why is this important?

- In what ways was Solomon's request a great *example to follow*? Read James 1:5. What assurance did James give in this verse? In addition to praying for wisdom, what other spiritual disciplines help us to acquire godly wisdom?

- In what ways does godly wisdom affect your everyday choices? In recent decisions, how have you been influenced by worldly or godly wisdom?

- Is there any area in your life today where we can pray for God to give you wisdom?

PRAYER:

Let's pray for one another today in that specific area of our lives where we need godly wisdom.

PRAYER REQUESTS:

BI-MONTHLY MISSION PROJECT NOTES:

WEEK 38

Weekly Bible Reading: .... Stories from 1 Kings
Weekly Bible Study: .... 1 Kings 21:1-25

1 KINGS 17:1-24   [CIRCLE ONE: S P A C E]

Personal Study Notes: _____

_____

_____

_____

1 KINGS 18:1-46   [CIRCLE ONE: S P A C E]

Personal Study Notes: _____

_____

_____

_____

1 KINGS 19:1-21   [CIRCLE ONE: S P A C E]

Personal Study Notes: _____

_____

_____

_____

1 KINGS 21:1-29   [CIRCLE ONE: S P A C E]

Personal Study Notes: _____

_____

_____

_____

1 KINGS 22:1-53   [CIRCLE ONE: S P A C E]

Personal Study Notes: _____

_____

_____

_____

Read carefully one chapter of the Bible five days a week. In each chapter look for a . . .
Sin to Confess / **P**romise to Claim / **A**ttitude to Change / **C**ommand to Obey / **E**xample to Follow.

AHAB TAKES NABOTH'S VINEYARD
(1 KINGS 21:1-25)

WEEKLY ASSIGNMENTS:

Lead Prayer Time: _____

Tell the Story (Paraphrase): _____

Read the Text: _____

Facilitate Bible Study: _____

DISCUSSION QUESTIONS:

- What is one special thing you have always wanted but never been able to have? How does this make you feel?

- In our story, Ahab, King of Israel, wanted his neighbor's vineyard, but Naboth wouldn't let him have it. How did this make Ahab feel and in what very immature ways did he react (v. 1-4)? What is the difference between wanting something and coveting something?

  wanting something that is not yours to have

- What did Jezebel, Ahab's wife, say to him about the situation (v. 5-7)? What plot did Jezebel connive to take Naboth's vineyard for her husband (v. 8-14)? What part did Ahab play in this situation? What became of Naboth and his vineyard (v. 15-16)?

- Who was Elijah the Tishbite and what did the Lord instruct Elijah to do (v. 17-19)? What specific words of judgment was Elijah told to deliver to Ahab (v. 20-22)? What specific words of judgment did God have for Jezebel (v. 23-24)?

- Read 1 Kings 22:34-40. What became of Ahab? Read 2 Kings 9:30-37. What become of Jezebel?

- God said that Ahab "sold himself to do what was evil" (v. 25a). What does it mean to sell yourself to do evil? Why does it never pay to do evil?

- God said that Jezebel "incited" or "stirred up" Ahab to do evil (v. 25b). How can others incite us to do evil? How can we stir up one another to do good? Why is it important to have close relationships with others who stir us up to do good works and to be faithful to God?

- Why is coveting a dangerous *sin to confess*? Read Phil. 4:11. What secret had Paul "learned" that can help us overcome the sin of coveting? In what ways have your learned this secret in your own life?

PRAYER:

Let's pray for one another today to learn the secret of godly contentment.

Johnathon Cann
The Harbinger
The Paradigm

PRAYER REQUESTS:

BI-MONTHLY MISSION PROJECT NOTES:

WEEK 39

Weekly Bible Reading: . . . . Stories from 2 Kings
Weekly Bible Study: . . . . 2 Kings 2:1-15

2 KINGS 1:1-18   [CIRCLE ONE: S P A C E]
Personal Study Notes: _____
_____
_____
_____

2 KINGS 2:1-25   [CIRCLE ONE: S P A C E]
Personal Study Notes: _____
_____
_____
_____

2 KINGS 4:1-44   [CIRCLE ONE: S P A C E]
Personal Study Notes: _____
_____
_____
_____

2 KINGS 5:1-27   [CIRCLE ONE: S P A C E]
Personal Study Notes: _____
_____
_____
_____

2 KINGS 6:1-33   [CIRCLE ONE: S P A C E]
Personal Study Notes: _____
_____
_____
_____

Read carefully one chapter of the Bible five days a week. In each chapter look for a . . .
Sin to Confess / **P**romise to Claim / **A**ttitude to Change / **C**ommand to Obey / **E**xample to Follow.

ELIJAH TAKEN AND THE MANTLE PASSED
(2 KINGS 2:1-15)

WEEKLY ASSIGNMENTS:

Lead Prayer Time: _____

Tell the Story (Paraphrase): _____

Read the Text: _____

Facilitate Bible Study: _____

DISCUSSION QUESTIONS:

- Who is the most influential person in your life that has gone on to be with the Lord? What lasting impact did this person have on you?

- In our story, it was time for Elijah the prophet to go home to be with the Lord. What was the special relationship between Elijah and Elisha (v. 1-6)? In what ways had Elisha been a "disciple" of Elijah?

  Holy friendship

- On three occasions, at Gilgal, Bethel, and Jordan, Elijah asked Elisha to stay behind. Why do you think he did this and why do you think Elisha refused?

  *Elijah wanted to be alone with God
  Elisha still needed to learn from Elijah*

- What miracle took place when the two men came to the Jordan River (v. 7-8)? How many times in the Bible did God miraculously part a body of water for someone? What lesson is God teaching us in this? *(3)*

Let a double share of your spirit come to me

- What was Elisha's one request of Elijah before he was taken (v. 9-10)? Do you think this was an honorable request? Why or why not? _Elisha wanted to be as devoted to God as Elijah was. He wanted Elijah's legacy - He wanted the spirit of God that was in Elijah_

- How was Elijah taken to heaven (v. 11-12)? Who else was taken to heaven without seeing death? Will others be taken this way? If so, who?

- When Elisha took up the cloak or mantle of Elijah, what did this indicate (v. 13)? What did it imply when God parted the Jordan for Elisha as He had done for Elijah (v. 14)? In what ways are Elisha's actions an _example to follow_?

- When someone has discipled you, when is the time to "pick up the mantle?" What will be required of you? Are you ready? Why or why not?

- When you take up the mantle of spiritual leadership in faith and courage, what will God do for you? What are the consequences when new leaders refuse to take up the mantle? What good things happen when they do?

PRAYER:

Let's pray for one another to know when it's time to take up the mantle.

PRAYER REQUESTS:

BI-MONTHLY MISSION PROJECT NOTES:

WEEK 40

Weekly Bible Reading: .... Stories from 2 Kings
Weekly Bible Study: .... 2 Kings 7:3-11

2 KINGS 7:1-20   [CIRCLE ONE: S P A C E]
*Personal Study Notes:*_____
_____
_____
_____

2 KINGS 8:1-29   [CIRCLE ONE: S P A C E]
*Personal Study Notes:*_____
_____
_____
_____

2 KINGS 9:1-37   [CIRCLE ONE: S P A C E]
*Personal Study Notes:*_____
_____
_____
_____

2 KINGS 10:1-36   [CIRCLE ONE: S P A C E]
*Personal Study Notes:*_____
_____
_____
_____

2 KINGS 12:1-21   [CIRCLE ONE: S P A C E]
*Personal Study Notes:*_____
_____
_____
_____

Read carefully one chapter of the Bible five days a week. In each chapter look for a . . .
Sin to Confess / **P**romise to Claim / **A**ttitude to Change / **C**ommand to Obey / **E**xample to Follow.

A DAY OF GOOD NEWS
(2 KINGS 7:3-11)

WEEKLY ASSIGNMENTS:

Lead Prayer Time: _____

Tell the Story (Paraphrase): _____

Read the Text: _____

Facilitate Bible Study: _____

DISCUSSION QUESTIONS:

- What is the most dangerous and frightening situation you have ever been in? How did you respond in this situation?

- In our story, four lepers of Samaria are in a very dangerous situation. What was their situation and how did they respond (v. 3-4)? Do you think they made a wise decision? Why or why not?

- When they came to the camp of the Syrians, what had happened (v. 5-7)? What had God done to cause this to happen?

- God sovereignly watches over His people. Read 2 Kings 6:12-17. How are these two stories similar in nature? We can't always see the ways that God watches over us and cares for us, but how do we know that He does?

- What did the Lepers do at first when they realized the camp was abandoned (v. 8)? Afterward, why did they say, "We are not doing right" (v. 9)? What did they fear would happen to them if they did not do what was right?

- What kind of day did the Lepers say that it was? What great decision did they make about this day of "good news" (v. 10-11)? In what ways are the actions of these lepers a great *example to follow*?

- For each of us who have been saved by faith in Christ, how is today a day of good news? When we fail to share the good news of the Gospel with others, why are we not doing right?

- When is the last time you shared the good news of the Gospel with someone who was lost? How did it go? Why do you think we do not share the Gospel more regularly? How can we do better at this?

PRAYER:

Let's pray for one another to have an opportunity this week to share the Gospel and to have the courage to do right.

PRAYER REQUESTS:

BI-MONTHLY MISSION PROJECT NOTES:

WEEK 41

Weekly Bible Reading: .... Stories from 2 Kings
Weekly Bible Study: .... 2 Kings 20:1-11

2 KINGS 13:1-25   [CIRCLE ONE: S P A C E]

Personal Study Notes: _____

_____

_____

_____

2 KINGS 17:1-41   [CIRCLE ONE: S P A C E]

Personal Study Notes: _____

_____

_____

_____

2 KINGS 18:1-37   [CIRCLE ONE: S P A C E]

Personal Study Notes: _____

_____

_____

_____

2 KINGS 19:1-37   [CIRCLE ONE: S P A C E]

Personal Study Notes: _____

_____

_____

_____

2 KINGS 20:1-21   [CIRCLE ONE: S P A C E]

Personal Study Notes: _____

_____

_____

_____

Read carefully one chapter of the Bible five days a week. In each chapter look for a . . .
Sin to Confess / **P**romise to Claim / **A**ttitude to Change / **C**ommand to Obey / **E**xample to Follow.

THE HEALING OF KING HEZEKIAH
(2 KINGS 20:1-11)

WEEKLY ASSIGNMENTS:

Lead Prayer Time: _____

Tell the Story (Paraphrase): _____

Read the Text: _____

Facilitate Bible Study: _____

DISCUSSION QUESTIONS:

- Can you share about a time when you were really sick? How did it make you feel when others prayed for you? How did it make you feel to pray for yourself?

- In our story, Hezekiah, King of Judah, was sick to the point of death. What important person visited Hezekiah and what bad news did he have for him (v. 1)? What does it mean when the Lord tells you to "set your house in order?"

- How did Hezekiah respond to the message of Isaiah the prophet (v. 2-3)? In his prayer, what did Hezekiah remind the Lord about himself? Read 2 Kings 18:3-7. How do these words confirm the sincerity of Hezekiah's prayer?

- In what ways does Hezekiah's prayer reflect great faith in the power and goodness of God? When God sent Isaiah back to Hezekiah, what good news did he have for him (v. 4-7)?

- Why do you think Hezekiah requested for a sign to confirm that God would heal him (v. 8)? What specific sign did he request from the Lord (v. 9-11)? How is this particular sign an amazing testimony of the omnipotence of God?

- When people are sick, why is it always a good thing for us to pray for them? What kinds of things should we pray for them?

- God does not always heal the sick, but why do you think He sometimes chooses to heal them? Why is God still good even when He does not heal?

- Can you share about a time when God answered your prayers for someone who was sick? When a believer dies, why is this his or her ultimate healing?

PRAYER:

Let's pray today specifically for some people who we know that are sick and who need God's power and grace.

PRAYER REQUESTS:

BI-MONTHLY MISSION PROJECT NOTES:

WEEK 42

Weekly Bible Reading: .... Stories from 2 Kings
Weekly Bible Study: .... 2 Kings 22:8-20

2 KINGS 21:1-26

[CIRCLE ONE: S P A C E]

Personal Study Notes: _____

_____

_____

_____

2 KINGS 22:1-20

[CIRCLE ONE: S P A C E]

Personal Study Notes: _____

_____

_____

_____

2 KINGS 23:1-37

[CIRCLE ONE: S P A C E]

Personal Study Notes: _____

_____

_____

_____

2 KINGS 24:1-20

[CIRCLE ONE: S P A C E]

Personal Study Notes: _____

_____

_____

_____

2 KINGS 25:1-30

[CIRCLE ONE: S P A C E]

Personal Study Notes: _____

_____

_____

_____

Read carefully one chapter of the Bible five days a week. In each chapter look for a . . .
Sin to Confess / **P**romise to Claim / **A**ttitude to Change / **C**ommand to Obey / **E**xample to Follow.

THE BOOK OF THE LAW IS FOUND
(2 KINGS 22:8-20)

WEEKLY ASSIGNMENTS:

Lead Prayer Time: _____

Tell the Story (Paraphrase): _____

Read the Text: _____

Facilitate Bible Study: _____

DISCUSSION QUESTIONS:

- What is the most valuable personal possession you have ever lost? How did it make you feel when you lost it? Did you ever find it again?

- In our story, Hilkiah, the high priest, found the Book of the Law in the house of the Lord during the reign of righteous King Josiah. How does a nation or a people completely "lose" the Bible? How close do you think we are to losing God's Word in our nation today? How can we find it again?

- Where did Hilkiah find the Book of the Law (v. 8)? How can God's Word be in the House of the Lord and yet be lost there at the same time?

- When King Josiah first heard the words of the Book of the Law, what was his immediate response (v. 9-11)? What did he realize about his people and his nation (v. 12-13)?

- Who was Huldah and what great responsibility had God given her (v. 14)? What does this teach about the important role of godly women in God's work? What message from God did Huldah have for King Josiah (v. 15-20)?

- Read 2 Kings 23:24-25. With his heart convicted by God's Word, what drastic changes did Josiah make? In what ways is Josiah's model of godly leadership an *example to follow* for leaders today? What difference would it make to have more leaders like Josiah?

- Some people seem to get little out of reading the Bible, while the hearts of others are greatly convicted. What do you think makes the difference?

- In your life today, would you consider God's Word to be lost or found? How hungry are you for God's Word? What personal changes are you making to bring your life more in line with God's Word?

PRAYER:

Let's pray today for God to give us a greater hunger of His Word and hearts that are greatly convicted by His Word.

PRAYER REQUESTS:

BI-MONTHLY MISSION PROJECT NOTES:

WEEK 43

EZRA 1:1-11   [CIRCLE ONE: S P A C E]
*Personal Study Notes:*_____

_____

_____

_____

EZRA 3:1-13   [CIRCLE ONE: S P A C E]
*Personal Study Notes:*_____

_____

_____

_____

EZRA 4:1-24   [CIRCLE ONE: S P A C E]
*Personal Study Notes:*_____

_____

_____

_____

EZRA 5:1-17   [CIRCLE ONE: S P A C E]
*Personal Study Notes:*_____

_____

_____

_____

EZRA 6:1-22   [CIRCLE ONE: S P A C E]
*Personal Study Notes:*_____

_____

_____

_____

Read carefully one chapter of the Bible five days a week. In each chapter look for a . . .
Sin to Confess / **P**romise to Claim / **A**ttitude to Change / **C**ommand to Obey / **E**xample to Follow.

THE HISTORIC DECREE OF KING CYRUS
(EZRA 1:1-11)

WEEKLY ASSIGNMENTS:

Lead Prayer Time: _____

Tell the Story (Paraphrase): _____

Read the Text: _____

Facilitate Bible Study: _____

DISCUSSION QUESTIONS:

- What does the phrase "twist of fate" mean? Can you share about a time when you experienced a sudden twist of fate?

- In our story, the Jewish exiles in Babylon had a sudden twist of fate when Babylon fell and the decree of King Cyrus of Persia set them free (538 BC). According to Ezra, what caused King Cyrus to do this (v. 1)? Read Proverbs 21:1. How does this verse apply to King Cyrus?

- According to Ezra, what great prophet of Judah had foretold of this? Read Jeremiah 29:10-11. What was God's promise in Jeremiah's prophecy? How is King Cyrus' decree a demonstration of God's faithfulness and sovereignty?

- What did King Cyrus say that the Lord God of heaven had done for him (v. 2)? What did he say that the Lord had charged him to do? Read Daniel 6:25-28. What possible influence might Daniel have had over King Cyrus?

- According to King Cyrus, how were the resources to be raised for the construction of the new temple (v. 3-4)? What is the difference between a "freewill offering" and "the tithe?" When God's work needs to be done, why should God's people be willing to give both the tithe and freewill offerings?

- According to Ezra, God "stirred up the spirit" of King Cyrus (v. 1) and He "stirred the spirit" of the first group of exiles to go rebuild the temple (v. 5-11). Can you share about a time when God "stirred up your spirit" to do something for Him? What is He is stirring your spirit about today?

- As an attitude to change, what can we learn from this story about keeping the faith even when life is hard? Can someone share of a time when the Lord God of heaven rescued you from a difficult situation?

PRAYER:

Let's pray for one another today to never lose faith even when life is hard.

PRAYER REQUESTS:

BI-MONTHLY MISSION PROJECT NOTES:

WEEK 44

Weekly Bible Reading: .... Stories from Nehemiah
Weekly Bible Study: .... Nehemiah 1:1-11

NEHEMIAH 1:1-11   [CIRCLE ONE: S P A C E]
Personal Study Notes: _____

_____

_____

_____

NEHEMIAH 2:1-20   [CIRCLE ONE: S P A C E]
Personal Study Notes: _____

_____

_____

_____

NEHEMIAH 4:1-23   [CIRCLE ONE: S P A C E]
Personal Study Notes: _____

_____

_____

_____

NEHEMIAH 5:1-19   [CIRCLE ONE: S P A C E]
Personal Study Notes: _____

_____

_____

_____

NEHEMIAH 6:1-19   [CIRCLE ONE: S P A C E]
Personal Study Notes: _____

_____

_____

_____

Read carefully one chapter of the Bible five days a week. In each chapter look for a . . .
Sin to Confess / **P**romise to Claim / **A**ttitude to Change / **C**ommand to Obey / **E**xample to Follow.

NEHEMIAH PRAYS FOR HIS PEOPLE
(NEHEMIAH 1:1-11)

WEEKLY ASSIGNMENTS:

Lead Prayer Time: _____

Tell the Story (Paraphrase): _____

Read the Text: _____

Facilitate Bible Study: _____

DISCUSSION QUESTIONS:

- Do you consider yourself to be a leader? Why or why not? Not everyone is a born leader, but do you think everyone can become one? Why or why not?

- In our story, God begins to rise up a great leader named Nehemiah whose heart was stirred for a righteous cause. What bad news did Nehemiah hear from his brother and what righteous cause stirred his heart (v. 1-3)? What was Nehemiah's first reaction to his brother's words (v. 4)?

  [handwritten: walls down gates burned / to help]
  [handwritten: sat down and cried - did not eat for several days]

- How is Nehemiah's response different from one of apathy and indifference? Why are feelings of apathy and indifference a much needed *attitude to change* for many people today? Why is indifference a *sin to confess*?

  [handwritten: no emotion / lack of concern]
  [handwritten: willing to go instead of staying in his comfort zone]
  [handwritten: she was brought to tears - he prayed for several days instead of eating because he was so concerned]

M M M a
several days *4 months*

- How long did Nehemiah fast and pray over his concern for Jerusalem? What is the spiritual discipline of "fasting?" Why is fasting important for us today? When should we fast? Can someone share a testimony about fasting?

great and awesome

- In Nehemiah's great prayer, what words of adoration did he speak to God (v. 5)? What words of confession did he speak to God (v. 6-7)? What words of Scripture did he call to God's remembrance (v. 8-9)? What specific things did he request (v. 10-11a)? How does your prayer life compare to Nehemiah's?

hear his request to with him to talk to king

sinned against you - not followed laws of moses

If you sin I will scatter you But if you return to me and obey my laws I will return you to Jerusalem

- What was Nehemiah's current occupation (v. 11b)? Based on Nehemiah's prayer request, what do you think it is that he desired to do? What must happen for the desires of Nehemiah's heart to become reality?

King's cup bearer

- What important lessons on leadership can we learn from Nehemiah? How are Nehemiah's actions *an example for us to follow*? What righteous cause is stirring your heart today? What are you going to do about it?

PRAYER:

Let's pray today that God will stir our hearts of a righteous cause and give us the faith and courage to take action.

unknown christian > *The Kneeling Christian*

PRAYER REQUESTS:

BI-MONTHLY MISSION PROJECT NOTES:

WEEK 45

Weekly Bible Reading: . . . . Stories from Nehemiah
Weekly Bible Study: . . . . Nehemiah 8:1-12

NEHEMIAH 8:1-18   [CIRCLE ONE: S P A C E]
Personal Study Notes: _____

_____

_____

_____

NEHEMIAH 9:1-25   [CIRCLE ONE: S P A C E]
Personal Study Notes: _____

_____

_____

_____

NEHEMIAH 9:26-38   [CIRCLE ONE: S P A C E]
Personal Study Notes: _____

_____

_____

_____

NEHEMIAH 10:28-39   [CIRCLE ONE: S P A C E]
Personal Study Notes: _____

_____

_____

_____

NEHEMIAH 13:1-31   [CIRCLE ONE: S P A C E]
Personal Study Notes: _____

_____

_____

_____

Read carefully one chapter of the Bible five days a week. In each chapter look for a . . .
Sin to Confess / **P**romise to Claim / **A**ttitude to Change / **C**ommand to Obey / **E**xample to Follow.

WORSHIPPING THE GREAT GOD
(NEHEMIAH 8:1-12)

WEEKLY ASSIGNMENTS:

Lead Prayer Time: _____

Tell the Story (Paraphrase): _____

Read the Text: _____

Facilitate Bible Study: _____

DISCUSSION QUESTIONS:

- How often do you join with others for worship? Do you think it is important for God's people to join together in worship? Why or why not?

- In our story, Nehemiah had led the Jewish people to re-build the walls around Jerusalem and afterward they gathered for worship. Where did they gather for worship and what does it mean that they gathered "as one man" (v. 1)?

- As they began to worship, what did Ezra the priest do before the assembly of men and women (v. 2)? How long did he read from the Book of the Law (v. 3)? What is the Book of the Law and why was it a central part of worship?

- Where was Ezra standing as he read the Book of the Law (v. 4-5a)? Why do you think the people stood up when he opened the Book of the Law (v. 5b)?

- During this time of worship, the people were active participants. In what different ways did the people respond and participate in worship (v. 6)? How are these worshippers an *example for us to follow*?

- Why is it important not only to read God's Word, but to also "give the sense of it" and help the people "to understand" it (v. 7-8)? Why do you think all the people wept as they heard the words of the law (v. 9)?

- Nehemiah exhorted the people to "not be grieved, for the joy of the Lord is your strength" (v. 10). What is the "joy of the Lord?" In what ways does the joy of the Lord give us strength? At the end of this worship service, why did the people go their way "rejoicing" (v. 11-12)?

- When you join with others for worship, do you come to participate or to evaluate? Do you come to give or receive? In what ways do you give and participate? From this study, how might your worship be different?

PRAYER:

Let's pray today for each of us to become more passionate worshippers.

PRAYER REQUESTS:

BI-MONTHLY MISSION PROJECT NOTES:

WEEK

ESTHER 1:1-22   [CIRCLE ONE: S P A C E]
Personal Study Notes: _____

_____

_____

_____

ESTHER 2:1-23   [CIRCLE ONE: S P A C E]
Personal Study Notes: _____

_____

_____

_____

ESTHER 3:1-15   [CIRCLE ONE: S P A C E]
Personal Study Notes: _____

_____

_____

_____

ESTHER 4:1-17   [CIRCLE ONE: S P A C E]
Personal Study Notes: _____

_____

_____

_____

ESTHER 5:1-14   [CIRCLE ONE: S P A C E]
Personal Study Notes: _____

_____

_____

_____

Read carefully one chapter of the Bible five days a week. In each chapter look for a . . .
Sin to Confess / **P**romise to Claim / **A**ttitude to Change / **C**ommand to Obey / **E**xample to Follow.

QUEEN ESTHER'S FAITH AND COURAGE
(ESTHER 4:1-17)

WEEKLY ASSIGNMENTS:

Lead Prayer Time: _____

Tell the Story (Paraphrase): _____

Read the Text: _____

Facilitate Bible Study: _____

DISCUSSION QUESTIONS:

- What do we dislike so much about a person who is a bully? When is the last time you had to deal with a bully and how did you deal with him or her?

- In our story, Queen Esther, the Jewish Queen of Persia, was called on to deal with a bully named Haman who plotted to destroy the Jews. Who was Mordecai and what was his relationship to Esther? What news had Mordecai learned that caused him great grief (v. 1-3)? How did he respond to this news?

- Who was Haman and why did he want to destroy all the Jews living in Persia? Throughout history, why do you think the Jewish people have often faced great persecution and threats of extermination?

- When Mordecai informed Esther about Haman's evil plot, what concern did she have about taking action (v. 4-11)? What words of encouragement did Mordecai share with her that inspired Esther to take action (v. 12-14)?

- What did Esther request of Mordecai and all the Jews living in Susa before she would appear before the King (v. 15-17)? How is Esther's wise request a great *example for us to follow*?

- Why is it important for all of us to have "a Mordecai" in our lives who encourages us to live with faith and courage? Can you share about someone in your life that has been a spiritual encourager to you?

- Mordecai told Esther that she might have come to the kingdom "for such a time as this" (v. 14). Do you believe that God sovereignly places you at certain places in certain times for certain reasons? Why or why not?

- At this season of your life, what do you think is God's plan for your life?

PRAYER:

Let's pray today that God will clearly reveal His plans for each of us and give us the faith and courage to act on His plans.

PRAYER REQUESTS:

BI-MONTHLY MISSION PROJECT NOTES:

WEEK 47

ESTHER 6:1-13   [CIRCLE ONE: S P A C E]

Personal Study Notes: _____

_____

_____

_____

ESTHER 7:1-10   [CIRCLE ONE: S P A C E]

Personal Study Notes: _____

_____

_____

_____

ESTHER 8:1-17   [CIRCLE ONE: S P A C E]

Personal Study Notes: _____

_____

_____

_____

ESTHER 9:1-32   [CIRCLE ONE: S P A C E]

Personal Study Notes: _____

_____

_____

_____

ESTHER 10:1-3   [CIRCLE ONE: S P A C E]

Personal Study Notes: _____

_____

_____

_____

Read carefully one chapter of the Bible five days a week. In each chapter look for a . . .
Sin to Confess / **P**romise to Claim / **A**ttitude to Change / **C**ommand to Obey / **E**xample to Follow.

SLEEPLESS IN PERSIA
(ESTHER 6:1-13)

WEEKLY ASSIGNMENTS:

Lead Prayer Time: _____

Tell the Story (Paraphrase): _____

Read the Text: _____

Facilitate Bible Study: _____

DISCUSSION QUESTIONS:

- What do you usually do when you cannot sleep at night? Do you have any special remedies to try to help you sleep?

- In our story, a sleepless night for King Ahasuerus of Persia resulted in a great blessing for Mordecia the Jew. On that night when King Ahasuerus could not sleep, what did he give orders for his servants to do (v. 1)?

- As the king's servants read from the "book of memorable deeds," what special deed did they read about Mordecia the Jew (v. 2)? What question did the king raise concerning Mordecia's heroic deed (v. 3)?

- When Haman entered the king's court, for what reason was he there to speak with the king (v. 4)? Before Haman could speak, what question did the king ask him (v. 5-6)? Who do you think Haman thought the king wanted to honor?

- What did Haman suggest should be done for the man whom the king delights to honor (v. 7-9)? What do you think Haman was thinking when he was required to honor Mordecia the Jew (v. 10-13)? Read Esther 7:7-10. What happened to Haman and what "irony" do you see in this?

- In this story, how far back and in what ways can you trace the sovereignty of God? In what good ways did God's sovereignty work in Mordecai's favor? In what tragic ways did God's sovereignty work against Haman's evil plot?

- What does it mean when we speak of "God's providence?" What great lessons can we learn from this story about the providence of God? In what ways does this story present us with a promise to claim?

- Can you share a testimony of a time you witnessed God's providence in your own life? How does the assurance of God's providence make you feel today?

PRAYER:

Let's pray today for faith to trust in God's providential care for our lives.

PRAYER REQUESTS:

BI-MONTHLY MISSION PROJECT NOTES:

WEEK 48

Weekly Bible Reading: ....Stories from Job
Weekly Bible Study: .... Job 19:13-27

JOB 1:1-22
[CIRCLE ONE: S P A C E]

Personal Study Notes: _____

_____

_____

_____

JOB 2:1-13
[CIRCLE ONE: S P A C E]

Personal Study Notes: _____

_____

_____

_____

JOB 19:1-29
[CIRCLE ONE: S P A C E]

Personal Study Notes: _____

_____

_____

_____

JOB 38:1-41
[CIRCLE ONE: S P A C E]

Personal Study Notes: _____

_____

_____

_____

JOB 42:1-17
[CIRCLE ONE: S P A C E]

Personal Study Notes: _____

_____

_____

_____

Read carefully one chapter of the Bible five days a week. In each chapter look for a . . .
Sin to Confess / **P**romise to Claim / **A**ttitude to Change / **C**ommand to Obey / **E**xample to Follow.

I KNOW THAT MY REDEEMER LIVES
(JOB 19:13-27)

WEEKLY ASSIGNMENTS:

Lead Prayer Time: _____

Tell the Story (Paraphrase): _____

Read the Text: _____

Facilitate Bible Study: _____

DISCUSSION QUESTIONS:

- What do you think are the most painful experiences people go through in life? Why are such painful experiences a true test of our faith?

- In our story, Job was passing through many painful experiences, but he continued to profess his faith in God. In addition to the loss of his children and his health, what other painful experiences did Job describe (v. 13-24)?

- How does it feel when even those whom we thought of as "intimate friends" turn against us and betray us? When we have a friend going through a painful experience, why is it important for us to draw near to him or her?

- When someone we know and love is passing through a difficult time, what kind of things should we do to show our love and support? Can you share about a time like this when someone was there for you?

- Even as Job recounted all the pain he was going through, what powerful profession of faith did he speak (v. 25)? In what way is God our "Redeemer?" When will God "stand upon the earth?" How do you think Job knew this?

- Even if God did not heal him physically, what did Job say that his eyes would see (v. 26-27)? In times of suffering, in what ways does Job give us *an example to follow*?

- Why is it important for our faith to be tested? What do trials prove about our faith--one way or another? Read 1 Peter 1:6-7. What happens when our faith is tested and proven to be genuine? What can we know about Job's faith?

- Can you share about a time when your faith was tested and about the spiritual growth you experienced in return?

PRAYER:

Let's pray today for someone we know who is going through a painful experience, that his or her faith will grow through the trial.

PRAYER REQUESTS:

BI-MONTHLY MISSION PROJECT NOTES:

WEEK 49

Weekly Bible Reading: .... Stories from the Prophets
Weekly Bible Study: .... Isaiah 53:1-12

ISAIAH 6:1-13   [CIRCLE ONE: S P A C E]
Personal Study Notes: _____
_____
_____
_____

ISAIAH 40:1-31   [CIRCLE ONE: S P A C E]
Personal Study Notes: _____
_____
_____
_____

ISAIAH 53:1-12   [CIRCLE ONE: S P A C E]
Personal Study Notes: _____
_____
_____
_____

JEREMIAH 1:1-19   [CIRCLE ONE: S P A C E]
Personal Study Notes: _____
_____
_____
_____

JEREMIAH 7:1-34   [CIRCLE ONE: S P A C E]
Personal Study Notes: _____
_____
_____
_____

Read carefully one chapter of the Bible five days a week. In each chapter look for a . . .
Sin to Confess / **P**romise to Claim / **A**ttitude to Change / **C**ommand to Obey / **E**xample to Follow.

OUR SUFFERING SERVANT
(ISAIAH 53:1-12)

WEEKLY ASSIGNMENTS:

Lead Prayer Time: _____

Tell the Story (Paraphrase): _____

Read the Text: _____

Facilitate Bible Study: _____

DISCUSSION QUESTIONS:

- What is a prophet? What important role did prophets play in the Bible?

- In our story, Isaiah the Prophet gave a clear description of Jesus' suffering and death hundreds of years before He was born. What did the prophet say about Jesus' personal appearance (v. 1-2)? How did he say that others would view Him (v. 3)? In what ways were these things true concerning Jesus?

- What did Isaiah say Jesus would do with our griefs and sorrows (v. 4)? In what ways did Jesus do this? Why did he say that Jesus would be "pierced and crushed" and what did he say about His "wounds or stripes" (v. 5)?

- In what way did the prophet say we are all like sheep (v. 6)? Do you agree or disagree? When did the Lord lay on Jesus "the iniquity of us all?" In what way is this a *promise to claim*? Do you think most people understand this?

- Read Matt. 26:63; 27:12-14. How do these words of Matthew fit Isaiah's description of Jesus? Why do you think Jesus remained silent before His accusers (v. 7)? If Jesus was "cut off out of the land of the living," how was it possible for God to "prolong His days" (v. 8-10)?

- Why did it please the Lord to "crush" Jesus and "put Him to grief" (v. 10-12)? What does this say about God's love for us? With such details given so long ago about Jesus' death and resurrection, what does this say about the Bible?

- In light of this prophesy, how is it possible that people do not believe in Jesus as Messiah and Savior? How could you use this passage to witness to someone who is lost? Knowing that Jesus suffered and died for you, in what way is your life an expression of gratitude to Him?

PRAYER:

Let's pray today giving thanks to Jesus for His great sacrifice for us and pray that our lives will be a reflection of our gratitude to Him.

PRAYER REQUESTS:

BI-MONTHLY MISSION PROJECT NOTES:

WEEK 50

Weekly Bible Reading: . . . . Stories from the Prophets
Weekly Bible Study: . . . . Ezekiel 37:1-14

JEREMIAH 18:1-23 [CIRCLE ONE: S P A C E]

Personal Study Notes: _____

_____

_____

_____

JEREMIAH 23:1-40 [CIRCLE ONE: S P A C E]

Personal Study Notes: _____

_____

_____

_____

JEREMIAH 32:1-44 [CIRCLE ONE: S P A C E]

Personal Study Notes: _____

_____

_____

_____

EZEKIEL 33:1-33 [CIRCLE ONE: S P A C E]

Personal Study Notes: _____

_____

_____

_____

EZEKIEL 37:1-28 [CIRCLE ONE: S P A C E]

Personal Study Notes: _____

_____

_____

_____

Read carefully one chapter of the Bible five days a week. In each chapter look for a . . .
Sin to Confess / **P**romise to Claim / **A**ttitude to Change / **C**ommand to Obey / **E**xample to Follow.

THE VALLEY OF DRY BONES
(EZEKIEL 37:1-14)

WEEKLY ASSIGNMENTS:

Lead Prayer Time: _____

Tell the Story (Paraphrase): _____

Read the Text: _____

Facilitate Bible Study: _____

DISCUSSION QUESTIONS:

- Do you ever go through times of spiritual dryness? Why do you think this happens?

- In our story, Ezekiel the Prophet was led by the Spirit to a certain valley. What did he see in the middle of the valley (v. 1-2)? What question did God ask him about these dry bones (v. 3a)? How did Ezekiel respond (v. 3b)?

- What did God tell Ezekiel to say to the dry bones (v. 4)? When these dry bones hear the word of the Lord, what did God say He would do for them (v. 5-6)? How is it possible for someone to listen to the Word of God but to not really "hear" it? In what ways would this contribute to spiritual dryness?

- What happened to the dry bones after Ezekiel prophesied over them (v. 7-8)? What one thing was still lacking in these bones (v. 9-10)? What do you think the "breath" symbolizes in this story?

- What did God tell Ezekiel that these dry bones represented (v. 11-14)? In what ways has this been fulfilled in the nation of Israel? Just as the house of Israel was spiritually dead and needed new life, in what ways is this true of our nation today?

- What does the word "revival" mean? According to this story, what is needed for God's people to experience a true spiritual revival? What great things happen when revival occurs?

- When you go through times of personal spiritual dryness, what lessons can you learn from this story? In what ways does Ezekiel provide *an example to follow* in times of dryness?

PRAYER:

Let's pray today for spiritual revival in our land and that revival will begin in each of us.

PRAYER REQUESTS:

BI-MONTHLY MISSION PROJECT NOTES:

WEEK 51

Weekly Bible Reading: .... Stories from the Prophets
Weekly Bible Study: .... Daniel 6:1-28

DANIEL 1:1-21   [CIRCLE ONE: S P A C E]
Personal Study Notes: _____
_____
_____
_____

DANIEL 3:1-30   [CIRCLE ONE: S P A C E]
Personal Study Notes: _____
_____
_____
_____

DANIEL 5:1-31   [CIRCLE ONE: S P A C E]
Personal Study Notes: _____
_____
_____
_____

DANIEL 6:1-28   [CIRCLE ONE: S P A C E]
Personal Study Notes: _____
_____
_____
_____

DANIEL 9:1-27   [CIRCLE ONE: S P A C E]
Personal Study Notes: _____
_____
_____
_____

Read carefully one chapter of the Bible five days a week. In each chapter look for a . . .
Sin to Confess / **P**romise to Claim / **A**ttitude to Change / **C**ommand to Obey / **E**xample to Follow.

DANIEL AND THE LION'S DEN
(DANIEL 6:1-28)

WEEKLY ASSIGNMENTS:

Lead Prayer Time: _____

Tell the Story (Paraphrase): _____

Read the Text: _____

Facilitate Bible Study: _____

DISCUSSION QUESTIONS:

- What is the worst you have ever been persecuted or mistreated because of your faith? How did you respond in this situation?

- In our story, Daniel was cast into a den of hungry lions because he refused to stop praying to his God. Why did the high officials of Persia seek to find a ground for complaint against Daniel (v. 1-4)? What was the only complaint they could find against him (v. 5)? What does this tell us about Daniel?

- What did the high officials of Persia request of King Darius to set a trap for Daniel (v. 6-7)? How did the king respond to their request (v. 8-9)? Why do you think unbelievers seem to delight in seeing godly people fall?

- When Daniel knew that the king had signed the ruling against prayer, what was his response (v. 10-13)? In what ways is Daniel's response similar to that of Shadrach, Meshach, and Abednego in Daniel 3? What example to follow do we see in these stories? How does godly courage strengthen our witness?

- What happened to Daniel when he was cast into the den of lions (v. 14-23)? In Daniel 3, what happened to Daniel's friends when they were cast into the fiery furnace? How did King Darius respond to Daniel's miraculous deliverance (v. 24-28)?

- In what ways do faith and courage go together? What positive things can happen when believers are persecuted for their faith? Why is it important for us to live with faith and courage today?

- How courageously are you living for God in your life right now? If you were to face a similar situation as Daniel and his friends, how do you think you would respond? In what areas of your life do you need more faith and courage?

PRAYER:

Let's pray for one another today to grow in faith and courage as we face the challenges of living for God in this world.

PRAYER REQUESTS:

BI-MONTHLY MISSION PROJECT NOTES:

WEEK 52

Weekly Bible Reading: .... Stories from the Prophets
Weekly Bible Study: .... Jonah 1:1-17

JONAH 1:1-17 [CIRCLE ONE: S P A C E]
*Personal Study Notes:*_____
_____
_____
_____

JONAH 2:1-10 [CIRCLE ONE: S P A C E]
*Personal Study Notes:*_____
_____
_____
_____

JONAH 3:1-10 [CIRCLE ONE: S P A C E]
*Personal Study Notes:*_____
_____
_____
_____

JONAH 4:1-10 [CIRCLE ONE: S P A C E]
*Personal Study Notes:*_____
_____
_____
_____

MALACHI 3:1-18 [CIRCLE ONE: S P A C E]
*Personal Study Notes:*_____
_____
_____
_____

Read carefully one chapter of the Bible five days a week. In each chapter look for a . . .
Sin to Confess / **P**romise to Claim / **A**ttitude to Change / **C**ommand to Obey / **E**xample to Follow.

JONAH AND THE GREAT FISH
(JONAH 1:1-17)

WEEKLY ASSIGNMENTS:

Lead Prayer Time: _____

Tell the Story (Paraphrase): _____

Read the Text: _____

Facilitate Bible Study: _____

DISCUSSION QUESTIONS:

- Have you ever tried to run away from something that God wanted you to do? If so, why did you run from God and how did that work out for you?

- In our story, God called Jonah to preach in Nineveh, but he rose to flee to Tarshish. Why do you think Jonah rose to flee from the presence of the Lord (v. 1-3)? Is it possible to flee from the Lord? Why or why not?

- What did God cause to happen to the ship carrying Jonah to Tarshish (v. 4)? How did the mariners on the ship respond to the storm (v. 5)? Why do you think Jonah was able to sleep during the storm (v. 6)? In what positive ways does God use the storms of life to accomplish His will in the lives of His children?

- How did the mariners find out that Jonah was the reason for the storm (v. 7)? What did Jonah instruct the mariners to do to him to quiet the storm (v. 8-12)? What signs are there that Jonah may have been depressed? What are some constructive ways for a believer to deal with sadness or depression?

- What happened to Jonah after he was cast into the sea (v. 13-17)? How long was Jonah in the belly of the fish and how did this change his attitude toward God? Is there a need for an attitude to change in your own heart concerning a specific area of God's will for your life? Can you share about it?

- When we know someone who is running from God, what can we do to help this person? How should we pray for him or her?

- What can we learn from this story about the power and sovereignty of God? Read Matt. 12:40. What is the relationship between the stories of Jonah and Jesus? If God rules over the wind, the fish, and the grave, what reason do you have to question His will for your life?

PRAYER:

Let's pray today that each of us will be fully obedient to God's will.

PRAYER REQUESTS:

BI-MONTHLY MISSION PROJECT NOTES:

AUTHOR BIO

Dr. Bill Wilks is Lead Pastor of NorthPark Church in Trussville, AL, where he has had the joy of serving since 1999.

He has a Doctor of Ministry degree from Southwestern Baptist Theological Seminary and frequently serves as an Adjunct Professor at the New Orleans Baptist Theological Seminary extension center in Birmingham, AL.

He is married to Rondie, and is the proud father of Josh, Jake, and Jared. Dr. Wilks is passionate about living a lifestyle of discipleship and equipping others to live the *D-Life*.

Contact Dr. Wilks for leadership training for *D-Life* at bill.wilks@ me.com. For additional help and encouragement for using and living the *D-Life*, check out:

- *The D-Life Website*: www.livethedlife.com
- *The D-Life Blog*: www.livingthedlife.com/category/d-life-blog/
- *Living the D-Life Facebook*: www.facebook.com/livingthedlife
- *Twitter*: www.twitter.com/BillWilks

CPSIA information can be obtained
at www.ICGtesting.com
Printed in the USA
LVHW011119190620
658111LV00004B/468

9 781632 040794